ADVANCE PRAISE

"This inspiring book shows how it's possible for people who have been cast aside in society to turn their lives around and start giving back to society. Catherine Hoke proves that within America's broken criminal justice system lies the potential for prisoners to become productive entrepreneurs and upstanding citizens. She writes with such passion that you'll want to open your calendar—or your wallet—to support this important cause."

ADAM GRANT
New York Times **Bestselling Author of** *Give and Take,*
Originals, **and** *Option B* **with Sheryl Sandberg**

"Catherine Hoke's story, *A Second Chance*, is a powerful reflection on the personal challenges she faced while devoting her life to tackling the systemic issues of America's criminal justice system and ending the epidemic of mass incarceration."

VALERIE JARRETT
Former Senior Advisor to President Obama

"In Silicon Valley, a second chance can be the key to achieving real innovation and progress. That's equally true for people serving time in prison — and why Cat's work creating life-changing second chances through entrepreneurial training programs within our criminal justice system is so necessary and worth supporting."

REID HOFFMAN
Co-founder of LinkedIn and Co-author of the #1 NYT
bestsellers *The Alliance* **and** *The Startup of You*

"This is the bravest book I have read in years."

BILL HYBELS
Founder of Willow Creek Church
and the Global Leadership Summit

"Cat Hoke is a force of nature. A Second Chance embodies every ounce of her, as it takes you on her personal journey, sharing her own second chance and the remarkable story and impact of Defy Ventures.

Twenty years from now, we will look back and say Cat and Defy helped transform millions of incarcerated people's hustles, providing a huge positive contribution to both their lives and the U.S. criminal justice system. This book is a roadmap, not only for our prison system, but also for your own personal journey, and is an inspiration for us all."

BRAD FELD
Partner, Foundry Group

"Catherine Hoke does important and inspiring work and is a personal inspiration to me. As described in her honest and moving new book, Defy harnesses human redemption in a way that allows people to simultaneously empower themselves and better our world. It will change your perspective; it will expand both your mind and your heart. It will prove to you that everyone deserves a second chance."

PREET BHARARA
Former U.S. Attorney
for the Southern District of New York

"Catherine is one of the most amazing people I have ever met. A pioneer of prison reform, Catherine is conquering uncharted territories based on a sincerely-held belief that everyone deserves a second chance. With exuberance and passion, she gives hope and instills discipline and self-confidence amongst the incarcerated."

ROSEMARY NDOH
Warden, Avenal State Prison

"Cat's story is remarkable. In my three decades of experience in corrections I've seen hundreds of programs, but Defy is unique in its recidivism reduction outcomes and engagement of the outside world. It's crucial that we find ways to harness the human potential of people in prisons and allow them to maximize this potential when they get out. If we are going to change the correctional system and increase public safety, we need new ways of thinking and bold action. Cat brings both!"

DAN PACHOLKE
Former Secretary,
Washington State Department of Corrections

"Catherine Hoke is a force to be reckoned with. Genuine, emotional, funny, and so very in your face; both in life and in her book. Cat weaves a tale of her personal journey and the Defy journey into a powerful story of how taking risks, embracing failure, becoming honest, and doing the really hard work will lead to meaningful success and a true sense of purpose. She captures transformational moments in the lives of the people she works with, using their stories to illustrate the incredible talent and wisdom contained within our prison systems. Cat's willingness to share her own fears and doubts strengthens the message that everyone deserves a second chance, and maybe even a third. This isn't a book about helping inmates become business owners; it is about people finding the courage to reach their full potential."

SCOTT FRAKES
Director, Nebraska Department of Correctional Services

"At the heart of every entrepreneur is a quest for better. Cat Hoke has unlocked this within the prison system, forging an entrepreneurial path to rehabilitation and fulfillment. Bravo!"

BETH COMSTOCK
Former Vice Chair, GE

"I've never seen anything like Defy, and I've been in corrections for 31 years. Through Defy, Catherine has proven that hope is a cure for violence, even for those who have been labeled 'the worst of the worst.' Defy has changed the culture at my institution. If you're a warden, figure out how to get Defy. Catherine's book shows us all our shared humanity and gives hope to people who have made mistakes on both sides of the fence."

CLARK DUCART
Warden, Pelican Bay State Prison

"Catherine Hoke's programs transform potentially serial criminals into successful, law abiding leaders who enrich their communities. For those who are interested in reducing crime and giving people a second chance, this book has inspiring answers".

CHARLES KOCH
Chairman of the Board and CEO, Koch Industries Inc.

"In *A Second Chance*, Catherine Hoke weaves her remarkable story through the tangled web of one of America's biggest problems: mass incarceration and the criminal justice system. Inside America's prisons, Catherine discovers human resiliency, courage, and what she calls 'America's most overlooked talent pool.' Relentlessly optimistic, brutally honest, and commanding empathy and action, Catherine's book asks us all to 'step to the line,' find common ground, and build a more just and equitable world. Regardless of your political leaning, this story exemplifies some of the best qualities of the American spirit while combating its inherent, systemic issues. If you loathe injustice, believe in underdogs, and find inspiration in the transformation of lives and communities, *A Second Chance* is a must-read."

CORY BOOKER
United States Senator, New Jersey

"*A Second Chance* is one of the most gripping and influential books I have ever read. This book will change the way you look at other people (and our society) forever.

Catherine Hoke is one of the most important voices in America today. Her personal story, passion, work, and writing are changing the way we think about the fundamental structure of this country."

TOM RATH
Author, *Are You Fully Charged* and *StrengthsFinder 2.0*

"The best sign that you admire the work of an organization as not only critically important to society, but dear to your heart, is that two seconds after you hear about it you think to yourself, 'I wish I'd thought of that.' That's how I feel about Defy. Ingenious and life-giving. This book is not only a must-read but a must-do."

MILES MCPHERSON
Sr. Pastor, Rock Church

"Catherine shows us that regardless of our personal history, every human life has value and is worth investing in."

JOSÉ ZEILSTRA
CEO, Gender Fair

"Cat Hoke's innovative program is helping men and women 'transform their hustle,' move past their criminal histories, and build new lives. She and her team at Defy Ventures may have found the key that unlocks real and lasting change for people that many thought were beyond hope. She is re-imagining how we approach incarceration and is giving those she serves a real shot at a better future. We are thrilled she and Defy are devoting their talents to currently and formerly incarcerated 'entrepreneurs in training' here in Colorado."

JOHN HICKENLOOPER
Governor, Colorado

"The first time I went to prison as a guest of Defy Ventures I was scared as hell as I walked into the room of tattooed prisoners shouting a morning welcome to me. I had never spent time in a correctional facility nor had I knowingly come face-to-face with somebody who had been convicted of robbery or murder. For people like me who are privileged to have grown up with loving parents and a safe neighborhood, we likely all imagine what meeting somebody convicted of such a crime would be like. I couldn't have been more wrong.

Everything that happened that day changed my life and my outlook on our penal system in America. I realized that many of the people that I met were hurting from a life of having been mistreated since early childhood. I learned that many people in prison had been there since the time they first became men and many didn't remember any other way of life. They all had deeply personal stories of regret and feeling ashamed and desperately wanting a shot at redemption.

Cat Hoke provides that for thousands of men and women who thought they didn't deserve another chance. She restores that for the least privileged people in our society and offers them a second chance at healing their own personal wounds before accepting a responsible role in the world and a mission to serve others. Cat selflessly gives of herself by bearing her own wounds and mistakes and her own personal search for a second chance.

Whether or not you believe in the inherent goodness in humanity and that everybody deserves a second chance, buy this book and get to know the person that I proudly pronounce as the most inspirational person I know. Thank you, Cat, for giving everything you have and sharing your journey with the rest of us."

MARK SUSTER
Venture Investor, Upfront Ventures

"Recidivism is a cancer in our country's penal system. As Americans, we pride ourselves as being #1; yet we have lots of room for improvement when it comes to prison rehabilitation. Cat and Defy's commitment is to give the incarcerated a real chance, and they are doing exactly that.

I brought my entire college football team to prison with Cat, and it was a life-changing experience for my players and for me personally.

If you care about society, you have to read this book."

JOE MOGLIA
Chairman, TD Ameritrade
Head Football Coach, Coastal Carolina

"Cat Hoke's Defy Ventures is symbiotic of the reform taking place in California, and across the nation, in how to incarcerate human beings. Compassion and redemption instead of vengeance and punishment. Self-confidence and hope instead of shame and isolation. With an army of successful business executives and an unrelenting passion for second chances, Defy tackles head-on the trauma that so many inside our prison walls have endured. This book chronicles the transformative spirit that can be instilled in once-lost souls and the significant benefit that rehabilitation has on our communities, public safety, and prisons. The stories, including that of Ms. Hoke's, are strong testimonials that our prison systems can and should do something better than simply locking people away. This is a must-read for everyone striving to believe in the human spirit; incarcerated people, business leaders, the general public, and, perhaps most importantly, correctional professionals and politicians."

SCOTT KERNAN
Secretary of Corrections, California Department of
Corrections and Rehabilitation

"If Cat Hoke's powerful book *A Second Chance* teaches us anything, it is that we all need a second chance at some point along the way. Cat's gripping story of redemption gives each of us permission to forgive ourselves for the mistakes we've made in the past and move forward more resilient and stronger than ever. For anyone looking for a second chance, this captivating book is a must read."

DAVID HORNIK
Venture Investor, August Capital

"This is required reading. Cat Hoke's story challenges us to think differently about courage, resilience and resolve. You will emerge with a renewed sense of optimism that the best days are always ahead."

BILL MCDERMOTT
Global CEO of SAP and Best-selling Author

"What could be more patriotic than repaying your debt to society by starting a business and creating jobs? Thanks to Cat and Defy Ventures for renewing our hope in the American Dream."

CHRISTOPHER SACCA
Founder and Chairman, Lowercase Capital

"At Google, we employ a data-driven, human-focused approach to philanthropy. We look for nonprofits that use technology and innovation to move the needle in creating justice and economic opportunity. We couldn't be prouder supporters of Defy Ventures—not just financially, but also with the time and pro bono services donated by hundreds of Googlers. If you've been looking for a way to make a difference, to level the playing field, or to fight systemic bias, read A Second Chance. You will not only understand why Google continues to make big bets on Defy; you will be compelled to do your part in creating a world that works for everyone."

JACQUELLINE FULLER
President of Google.org

"Cat is spot on in her belief that people shouldn't solely be judged by the worst thing they've ever done. It was this way of thinking that allowed me to build one of the largest low-cost inmate service providers in the country after serving a 5-year federal prison sentence. Read this book and discover your own potential, regardless of your past."

FREDERICK HUTSON
Founder and CEO, Pigeonly

"In *A Second Chance*, Catherine Hoke poses a simple question: What if you were known only for the worst thing you've done? Millions of Americans are permanently defined by a past decision, for which they've served their time, rather than who they are today. Catherine's story is about redefining one's self, facing down seemingly impossible barriers, and igniting the human spirit through empathy, grit, and determination."

VAN JONES
Social Entrepreneur and Political Commentator

A SECOND CHANCE

The Domino Project
Published by Do You Zoom, Inc.

First hardcover edition February, 2018

For more information, address:

Defy Ventures
5 Penn Plaza, 19th Floor
New York, NY 10001
info@defyventures.org

For information about special discounts for bulk purchases,
please contact Defy Ventures Special Sales at info@defyventures.org.

Library of Congress Cataloging-in-Publication Data in progress.

Hoke, Catherine, 1977—
A Second Chance: For you, for me, and for the rest of us / Catherine Hoke
p. cm.
ISBN 978-0-9996695-0-1

FIRST EDITION

Book design by Alex Peck
Typeset in Garamond Premier Pro
Printed in the United States of America

10 9 8 7 6 5 4 3 2 1 § 18

A SECOND CHANCE

FOR YOU, FOR ME, AND FOR THE REST OF US

Catherine Hoke

FOUNDER, DEFY VENTURES

CONTENTS

FOREWORD

Sheryl Sandberg
Chief Operating Officer of Facebook

When I was working on my book *Option B* about building resilience in the face of adversity, I looked everywhere for the best real-life examples of resilience—people enduring a crushing challenge and finding strength and even joy as they fought to move forward.

Few stories moved me like Catherine Hoke's.

Catherine knows about resilience from the work that is her life's purpose: helping people with criminal histories start businesses so they can rebuild their lives. She knows about it from her own experience—she has made mistakes, felt profound shame, even questioned whether she deserved to live. And she knows about it from what happened after that—forgiving herself, picking herself up, and getting back to the work of serving others.

When I heard Catherine's story, I wanted to meet her. Earlier this year, I finally got the chance. She and I spent the day together at a Defy Ventures program in a California state prison, where I met the "entrepreneurs-in-training" she works with. Though many were serving time for serious crimes, it wasn't hard to feel empathy for them—nearly all had dealt with abuse and poverty from an early age, and they were all trying to turn their lives around.

What I didn't expect was that they would feel empathy for me, despite the privilege of my life. My husband, Dave, had died not long before and I was—and am still—devastated by it. These men shared their own stories of loss as well. The differences in our circumstances didn't stand in the way of our shared humanity. It was a reminder of how we can gain strength and wisdom from one another as we deal with life's challenges.

That insight is at the heart of Catherine's work. She believes that, with the right support, anyone can recover from anything. I've never been as inspired as I was that day at the prison. Catherine, her program, and the entrepreneurs-in-training were everything I had studied about resilience, come alive.

I used to think that we're born with a fixed amount of resilience. When I lost Dave, I desperately hoped that my kids and I would have enough to see us through. Then my friend Adam Grant, a psychologist, explained that I had it wrong. We don't have a fixed amount of resilience. It's a muscle we can build—in ourselves, in our children, and in our communities.

One of the key ways we build it is through self-compassion. Of everything I've learned from Catherine, that's the most important. It's one thing to feel compassion for others. It's often a lot harder to feel it for ourselves. We want to avoid self-pity and self-indulgence so we deny ourselves kindness and understanding when we make mistakes. And that can lead to shame—the feeling of being small and worthless—which in turn can lead to addiction, violence, and other forms of abuse.

It's a vicious cycle.

We break it by recognizing that our imperfections are part of being human ... that making a bad decision does not make us a bad person ... that we are more than the worst thing we've ever done ... and that we always have another chance to do something of value.

Catherine has spent years encouraging people in prison to believe this about themselves—within a system that often treats the incarcerated as less than human. After her mistakes, she had to work even harder to believe this about herself. She used her second chance to extend new second chances to others.

This book is the story of that journey. If you've ever wondered how to put your life back together after it's fallen apart—or how to find joy and self-worth again after it's been drained away—Catherine's book will show you how.

INTRODUCTION

Wrath seems to outweigh forgiveness these days. We're quick to anger, to expel, and most of all, to punish.

The thing is, when we express our wrath, it comes right back at us. And forgiveness, amazingly, does the same thing.

Cat Hoke is a prophet of forgiveness. Every day, she does the difficult work of looking our fear right in the eye—without blinking. Every day, she stands up, speaks up, and leads. And every day, she shows us a better path, a path lit by empathy, possibility, and belief.

This book, like Cat's work at Defy, will change you. It helps us see how powerful our ability to forgive is. Not just the ability to forgive others, but the ability to forgive ourselves.

Seth Godin
Hastings-on-Hudson, NY
December 2017

DEDICATION

I dedicate this book to the courageous men and women of Defy. You have my highest respect. For being the living proof that transformation and second chances are possible: thank you for being my reason to keep fighting.

I also dedicate this book to the thousands of generous funders of Defy who provide scholarships to our Entrepreneurs-in-Training (EITs): we would have nothing without you. Thank you for being bold ambassadors of grace and for putting your money where your mouth is when it comes to second chances.

One of our EITs in solitary confinement named Jesus wrote to a Defy volunteer: "I'm so used to the pain and disappointment that it doesn't bother me or hurt me. Yet the act of kindness you're doing for us hurt me in a good way. It made me feel emotions I haven't felt in years. I'm only 22, and the last time I felt those feelings, I was 11 or 12. Your act of kindness lets me know good people still exist."

I'm deeply grateful to our donors and volunteers for seeing value where others don't.

The events in this book actually happened, and the details are included to the best of my recollection.

THE WORST THING

I sat at my desk, finger on the Send button, cringing in front of the email I knew I had to send. It would destroy me and my career. But I didn't have a better option.

Filled with shame and self-hate, I sent it.

What would it be like if you were known only for the worst thing you've ever done?

In 2009, I was kicked out of the organization I had founded. I had spent the past five years working with the Texas prison system. I was thirty-one years old, just divorced, and in forty-eight hours, I was to become nationally known for a sex scandal. I was certain that for the rest of my life, I'd be known for what I'd done wrong instead of for the good work I had devoted my life to.

What happened to leaders like me who screwed up? Was there an island of castaways somewhere?

I believed I would never really live again. I had no vision for a future. I could see only clouds and darkness. No way out, no path to the other side of the depression.

In the swirl of scandal and shame, I never could have imagined my own second chance, an opportunity to transform my hustle. But today, I'm living my wildest dream. I lead Defy Ventures, a national prison rehabilitation program and incubator that transforms the hustle, and lives, of men, women, and youth with criminal histories.

We are second-chance entrepreneurs.

We are Entrepreneurs-in-Training (EITs).

We create healing and economic opportunities for our country's most overlooked talent pool—people who are voiceless because they are incarcerated and forgotten.

This is the story of how I got to the other side of my mess. More than that, it's a manifesto about how we can each learn from the journeys of the brave men and women who have found a second chance through Defy.

If you count yourself amongst us imperfect humans, hopefully this book will show you that you are *far* from alone. People with rap sheets that are "worse than yours" have not only bounced back, but have turned their pain into beauty. I want that for you.

Or maybe you're reading this because someone you love has screwed up. Maybe you want them to move forward and he or she isn't ready. Perhaps you want to learn how to help them get to the other side of the mess. Or maybe you aren't ready to forgive and to give someone a second chance, but you know that you want to. This book is for you, too.

If the people I serve can recover from grave mistakes, receive a second chance, and become the CEOs of their new lives, so can you.

THIS IS DEFY

Step to the line.

A long strip of duct tape stretches down the middle of the floor of the sweaty prison gym.

Our incarcerated EITs (Entrepreneurs-in-Training) stand on one side. Our volunteers (including many CEOs, entrepreneurs, and investors) are on the opposite side. EITs and volunteers stand inches away from each other, toes nearly at the line, staring each other dead in the eyes in intense silence.

"If the statement is true, you step to the line. Step to the line with your toes actually touching it. If it's not true, back up five feet. Let's see what we have in common, and let's respect our differences."

Who steps to the line?

"Step to the line if you've done arrestable things for which you haven't been arrested."

Ninety percent of our volunteers are at the line.

Would you be?

When I remind them that driving with one too many drinks in them, holding weed before they smoked it (at least up until recently), and even using someone else's open Wi-Fi network are felonies in many states, everyone is at the line.

"Step to the line if you've ever been in a physical fight to prove yourself—even dating back to your childhood."

Seventy percent of our volunteers—including many of our women volunteers—are at the line.

Would you be? Do you have family members who would be?

Every EIT is at the line.

"Step to the line if you've committed a violent crime."

Ninety-nine percent of our EITs are at the line. Almost no volunteers are at the line, until this:

"I said, step to the line if you've committed a violent crime. I didn't say 'convicted' of a violent crime."

A few volunteers shuffle forward.

"I must not be making myself clear. After the previous question, most of you were at the line for being in a physical fight to prove yourself. A physical fight is a violent crime."

The majority of volunteers step to the line, some of them with a "you've got to be kidding me" look.

"You think I'm being ridiculous by calling your playground fight 'violent crime.' Because maybe in your neighborhood, you got a timeout or got grounded for a few days. But my guys, like Justin? They started getting locked up as young as the age of seven. For what? For playground fights! For shoplifting when they were starving because mom and dad were nonexistent.

"Step to the line if your first arrest was before the age of ten." Half of our EITs are at the line.

"Step to the line if your first arrest was before age eight. Seven." Some of the EITs are still at the line.

"Why did you get locked up?"

For punching a boy who was picking on me.

At Defy, nearly all of our EITs have been convicted of violent crimes. These people are the ones that politicians write off as being unredeemable. Some progressive thinkers in rehabilitation have started advocating for the release of incarcerated people who have committed non-violent crimes, but most of society thinks my guys are unforgivable.

This book is the story of America's most "unforgivable" people redeeming their lives and achieving success. If they can live fulfilling lives after their bad decisions cost them decades, so can you.

"Eighteen months ago, I got a call from a Google executive who was a Defy donor and volunteer. This time, he needed my help. He had just gotten into a bar fight. A fistfight. He was facing ten years in prison for a violent crime. How much time do you think he got?"

The volunteers shout out their best guesses. My EITs are shaking their heads; they know the answer.

"He got zero years. He got community service. Because he is rich, and white, and has access, and paid his attorney more than $100,000 to fight his case.

"How many of you followed the case of the really cute Stanford swimmer, Brock Turner? He had blonde hair and blue eyes, and the judge sentenced him to only six months because apparently, Brock swam really, really fast and he had a bright future. Six months. For raping a girl. If he weren't so cute or so fast—or so white—he probably would have gotten life."

———

The physical representation, the moment of taking accountability, of seeing and being seen, of raw and painful humanity—this experience is a critical part of our mission. Shame washes away as people reveal their pasts. People *choose* forgiveness.

"To conclude the exercise, step to the line if this is true: 'I might not be able to explain it, but even though I've been revealing difficult things and have made myself vulnerable in this exercise, right here, right now, I feel safe, accepted, and loved.'"

Everyone is at the line.

"Let me get this straight. You feel safe, accepted, and loved—by people who were strangers two hours ago? Did you forget that you're in a maximum-security prison?"

People on both sides of the line whoop and holler and high-five. Partly because they just completed this soul-baring exercise. And partly because one of the most powerful things we can experience in life is to reveal our true selves, warts and all, and still be respected, appreciated, and loved—with non-judgmental love.

———

I'm not a criminologist, but in 12 years of doing this work, I've come to believe that the number-one reason that people recidivate (return to prison)—and often don't even give themselves a second chance—is that they lack a positive, legal vision. Many believe that no one will hire them and no one will want them. Many incarcerated people don't have many successful *legal* role models.

Even worse—incarcerated people often don't have the skills, training, experience, confidence, or résumés to land a job. I teach a course called "How to Write a Résumé When You've Served 19 Years in Prison." Most of my EITs were incarcerated by the age of twenty, and most have been incarcerated for ten to twenty years.

Imagine having to start your life over from scratch—never having held a legal job, never having seen the internet, never having had a dad to teach you how to tie a tie.

Imagine surviving the dehumanizing messages that would be pounded into your brain every day you're in prison—including the last one. On your way out of the gates on release day, you're told, "See you back here soon." That prophecy turns out to be correct 76.6 percent of the time.

More than three out of four people who walk out of prison walk back in some day.

Other messages that would reinforce your sense of hopelessness:

I told you that you were just like your father and that you'd end up in prison. (Seventy percent of children whose parents were incarcerated end up incarcerated.)

You're never going to amount to anything.

No one will ever hire you with that rap sheet; why try?

There's a decent chance that your family has given up on you and lost hope for your future. And the more years you serve, the less chance of a visit. You feel despised, shameful, and alone.

Here's how we describe our mission:

> *Defy transforms hustle. We maximize the potential of those impacted by the criminal justice system by building redemptive communities that pursue entrepreneurship and personal growth.*

> *Most people in prison are natural-born entrepreneurs who previously directed their hustling skillsets into illegal enterprises (mostly centered around selling drugs). Accomplished former drug dealers and gang leaders have a lot in common with successful CEOs and entrepreneurs.*

> *The big idea behind Defy: what if we transformed that hustle into legal entrepreneurship? How could our EITs, their children, our communities, and our country win if they went legit with their skills?*

Empathy and character development are at Defy's core. Our training leads to profound character and mindset shifts among EITs and shatters negative perceptions of people with criminal histories. Each EIT's success enables us to challenge stigmas that contribute to economic and racial injustice.

Take Coss Marte, who went to prison at 19. He was making $2 million a year in drug sales. He was convicted of a drug charge and served five years. When he went to prison, he was so unhealthy and overweight that he was told he would die there. After an altercation with a correctional officer, he was placed in solitary confinement. Coss came up with an innovative workout regimen and lost 70 pounds in six months. After he was released from "the hole" back to the prison yard, he led a group of 20 incarcerated men through his workout regimen, and they lost a thousand pounds collectively.

When Coss got out of prison, Defy's incubator provided him with the training, access, mentoring, and financing needed to turn his idea into a business. ConBody is a prison-style fitness boot camp, and if you go, you and your "cellie" will participate in bodyweight-bearing exercises. ConBody serves 5,000 customers a day. Coss has given a TEDx talk. He's had a seven-page spread in *Men's Fitness*. He's hired 15 people with criminal histories, including other Defy grads, as trainers. Through ConBodyLive.com, he has customers in 24 countries. Defy helped him raise $250,000 more from investors to scale his business.

Saks Fifth Avenue needed more foot traffic, so they built a ConBody gym *inside* the Manhattan department store.

Coss is making it. What do I love most about him? His financial bottom line is far from his only bottom line. Coss shows people on both sides of the fence that transformation is within reach. He's a powerful voice on prison reform. Coss also serves as a judge in our Shark Tank-style pitch competitions.

This month, Coss is joining me at Pelican Bay State Prison in California—the country's most notorious prison. We run Defy in Pelican Bay's solitary confinement facility (called the SHU, or Security Housing Unit). These guys get almost no access to rehabilitation, but they need it most, and they are among Defy's best EITs.

Pelican Bay has 1,200 SHU beds. SHU residents spend 22.5 hours a day alone in windowless cells about the size of a parking spot. The remaining 90 minutes? It's spent in a small, tall concrete box that is called an exercise "yard." They get no human contact and are fed through "feeding slots" in their door.

These men are not allowed contact visits from the outside. One of Defy's graduates did 32 years in the SHU. Thirty-two years. I can't wait for our incredibly devoted SHU guys to have their worlds rocked as they hear Coss's SHU-to-CEO success story.

NEW YORK STOCK EXCHANGE

We transform the hustle of our currently and formerly incarcerated EITs by offering intensive leadership training, business pitch competitions, executive mentoring, financial investment, and startup incubation.

About 70 percent of the training in Defy's program, called "CEO of Your New Life," centers on building a holistically fulfilling life and a "Generous Hustle." We have more than 100 courses that cover character development, recovery from depression, parenting, Emily Post etiquette, technology, job readiness, forgiveness, the Five Love Languages, communication, relationships, and more.

Ninety-five percent of Defy's EITs never return to prison. At less than five percent recidivism, I believe Defy has the lowest recidivism rate (for a program of scale).

We also have a 95 percent employment rate on average after our EITs are released from prison. Our grads get jobs from our executive volunteers, from EITs who have started businesses, and from organizations that know talent when they see it. They recognize that our EITs are deeply loyal and willing to prove themselves.

Why *wouldn't* a smart employer hire from America's most overlooked talent pool?

The employers win. The EITs win. Their kids win. Taxpayers win. America wins.

Do we cherry-pick EITs to get these results?

Thanks for asking. Take one look at our guys' rap sheets and then you tell me.

Wardens like to send us to their toughest yards with their most challenging populations because they know that "a man without hope is a dangerous thing." We admit every single person who applies, as long as we have the physical space and the funding. We know that all people are redeemable when they take ownership of their actions and are willing to reconcile their pasts so they can transform their futures.

Our EITs succeed because we give them a legitimate chance to succeed and we equip them to become profitable entrepreneurs, stellar employees, engaged parents, and committed role models and leaders with powerful voices of redemption. We intentionally build life-giving, authentic communities of EITs and thousands of grace-loving executive volunteers. They bond in their humanity.

Our staff and boards serve many other customers as well: EITs' children and families, correctional officials and officers, public officials, volunteers, donors, and taxpayers at large.

Aren't we all ex-somethings?

Society slaps plenty of negative labels that bind Defy's beneficiaries to their pasts. Our EITs pay their debts to society by serving their time. Why does our country, the "land of second chances," turn that time into a life sentence, even after release, with the invisible handcuffs of damaging stigmas?

Instead of referring to our EITs as ex-anythings, we focus on who they are today and who they're becoming.

We're Defy and we believe in second chances. Second chances for those who are caught and labeled, and for those who are still in hiding, being eaten alive by shame. I hope I can find them.

Maybe you're one of them.

By the way, everyone thinks we're in the second-chance business. We are. But if you knew my EITs' backstories, you might realize that we are more often in the legitimate-first-chance business. We're also in the third-chance business, and the thirty-third-chance business.

Because we all deserve a chance.

We unlock potential everywhere we find it.

I was created with rose-colored glasses that allow me to see potential. Not just for my EITs, but for you, too. Even when you don't see it for yourself. Even if you've done the "worst things ever."

You are not your past.

That's worth repeating: *You are not your past.*

Every single day, I see people who have been labeled as "monsters" reconcile their pasts, recover, and get second chances and new lives.

We're all behind bars—the bars of perfection, the bars of shame, of judging and being judged.

This book isn't an exhaustive manual on bouncing back from screw-ups. It won't apply to every situation, but I'm hoping that you'll find some clear parallels between my life, my EITs' lives, and your own.

Thank you for joining me on this journey and for daring to know us and our stories of pain and beauty. Watch out: you might even find some of your story in here as well.

MY STORY

I was 26 years old and living in Manhattan, working in private equity. One night I had a friend over for dinner. She was a J.P. Morgan executive. I shared with her my desire to find a greater purpose. There had to be more to life than just aiming to die with a big pile of money.

I was surprised when she invited me to prison. Not just any prison, but a Texas prison. Not just on any date, but over Easter weekend of 2004—the weekend for which I already had tickets to fly from New York City to California to be with my family.

"No thanks." I had every excuse to say no. I hated criminals, had never been to Texas, never cared to go to Texas, had family plans—and why the hell would I ever want to go to a prison?

But as she shared with me her passion for the work she was able to do in prison, I felt this buzz in my heart that was hard to ignore. She spoke in a language that resonated with me: underdogs, grace, second chances, injustice. No, not everyone in prison wants to transform, but so many do—and don't know where to turn.

To this day, I wonder, what if I had ignored my heart and kept the "no" a "no"?

My open heart for injustice and vulnerable populations came from my mom, who always wanted to pick up homeless people and bring them home to live with us. (My dad wasn't so into that idea.) But growing up, I wanted to be just like my dad. He gave me my love for underdogs, entrepreneurship, and crazy odds.

When he was 22 years old, my Hungarian-Yugoslav dad immigrated to Canada with $200 in his pocket. He became an electrical engineer, and he's been an inventor ever since; he's 73 now and is still inventing and filing technology patents like a madman.

One of my earliest childhood memories is of sitting around the family dinner table and hearing my dad say, "You have 60 seconds. Invent something." He had a countdown clock. I had to stand up, pitch an idea to my family, and explain what problem my invention would solve, why it was different, what it would cost, and how much demand there'd be. I was raised in a "Shark Tank."

I did this as young as six years old. I came up with lots of inventions, like running shoes that could fly. One thing I don't remember ever happening was having my idea get shot down; I was never told that my ideas couldn't work, regardless of how ridiculous my childish entrepreneurial fantasies may have been. The question was always, "How can you make that happen?" It was up to me to come up with creative solutions. I was given permission to attempt the impossible. And given permission to fail.

When I was 12 years old, a good friend of mine was brutally murdered by two 16-year-old boys. One boy got five years in prison. The other got ten years. To me, those sentences were an affront, a gross injustice. I thought both boys should rot and die in prison. I also used to be all about the death penalty. Eye for an eye—why not?

Although I'd never known anyone who had gone to prison, it was easy to extrapolate from my single experience and write off all incarcerated people. From that point forward, they weren't even people to me—they were wild, caged animals. Lock 'em up, throw away the key, and never look back.

As I grew up and learned about the costs of incarceration, my version of criminal justice only got more ruthless. I thought we should just fry them all; who cares if a few innocent ones suffer in the process? Coddling criminals felt like a ridiculous taxpayer burden with no real purpose.

Never mind the racial and economic biases and the sentencing disparities.

Never mind the prevalence of innocent people who are pressured into pleading guilty.

Never mind the all-white juries who sentence black men to 20 times the time that a white man would get for the same crime.

I was proud to be tough on crime. Just like politicians we all know.

My friend from J.P. Morgan was so persuasive that I switched my plane tickets and went to Texas instead of California for the Easter weekend. I thought I had essentially signed up to go on a zoo tour.

It was a three-day trip to visit four Texas prisons. The trip began at a women's prison, included a death row visit, and concluded at a Houston men's prison. As we entered the gates of the first prison, I was terrified.

My first conversations changed everything. I cried my way through the three days. Not because I felt sorry for the incarcerated people that I met, but because I felt sorry for myself. I couldn't believe the ugliness of my own heart, how ruthless I had been in writing people off as being less than human beings—people whose stories I hadn't known.

I don't think I'd ever been more face-to-face with my own ignorance.

What a hypocrite I was. As a self-proclaimed Christian, I was happy for the grace offered for *my* mistakes, but I had been completely unwilling to think about grace for people who had committed sins called worse than mine. I felt ashamed—and now knew I had to do something about it. Just as my ignorant eyes had been opened, I had to open the eyes of others so that these humans—my new friends behind bars—could be seen.

As I listened to one story after another that weekend, they blurred into one. The people I met had grown up being physically (and often sexually) abused; had been deserted by their fathers (or never met them in the first place); were handed their first drugs to sell at age thirteen; and had gotten jumped into a gang. Drug dealing and gang rivalry became their lives. It was no surprise to anyone that nearly all of the people I met were incarcerated by age 20.

I met a particularly charismatic guy named Johnny. When he was eight, he saw his dad get murdered—by his grandfather. If my dad had been murdered in front of me, I'm pretty sure I would have made choices that would have landed me in prison.

Empathy finally kicked in—so strong I felt like I was drowning in it.

Toward the end of that Easter weekend in Texas, I met a successful businessman and his wife. He ran a construction company. When I learned that he had done serious prison time, a light bulb came on.

In that first prison visit, I started the transformation of my own hustle into what I call my Generous Hustle. A Generous Hustle isn't selfish. Instead, the Generous Hustle is creating value by creating positive impact in the lives of others.

I realized that many (not all) drug dealers and gang leaders are entrepreneurs and proven business leaders. I learned that many gangs and drug rings have management teams, boards of directors, and bookkeepers. They run organizations that have better margins than most software companies. They create proprietary sales channels with incredibly high customer retention rates. They have a bottom-line mentality and face way tougher competition than legal businesses do.

The business component they lacked? Their risk management strategies. After all, they had been busted.

Many of the people I met had mastered the art of entrepreneurship and were more "accomplished" than many legal entrepreneurs I knew. But they were missing the other half, the Generous Hustle: the ability to see themselves as positive contributors to their communities.

What would happen if these incarcerated men were equipped to go legit with their hustling skills?

In my short venture capital and private equity career, I had been taught to recognize a good ROI opportunity. Before my eyes were America's greatest underdogs. They didn't seem to realize that they were capable of becoming law-abiding entrepreneurs, but I needed no convincing. I saw their potential and believed in the possibility to my core.

The guys I met consumed my heart. I couldn't wipe their faces out of my brain. I cried during the whole flight back to New York City.

The epiphany could have just ended at one inspirational weekend in Texas. But at the last prison I visited, the guys said to me, "Please come back." And I said, "I will."

Another thing my dad did for me: He taught me that "yes means yes." I was taught not to say polite niceties when I didn't mean them. So I was fully intent on upholding my promise to return.

When I got an unexpected invitation to return to Texas for a wedding, just a month later, it was a sign from God if I had ever seen one.

If I was hauling all the way back to Texas, surely I had to stop by the prison that had affected me most.

———

Sometime after that second trip to Texas, I realized that I could do more than visit. Maybe I could build an organization to work with the guys before and after their release. Maybe I could help them build a new future.

I realized that as long as we were labeling them (and they were labeling themselves) as "cons," we were all going to be victims of a never-ending cycle. So I began thinking of these people as entrepreneurs. I saw a chance to hustle with them and for them, to create a story that could break a cycle.

———

On May 24, 2004, Prison Entrepreneurship Program (PEP) was born. At the time, I thought it was just a "little project," not the birth of my new Generous Hustle and life journey.

I invited a handful of executives I knew to join me at the Texas prison on only two weeks' notice. I didn't know people in Texas, so when these investors and CEOs agreed to fly to Houston, to come to a prison, I could hardly believe it.

I thought, "Maybe I'm on to something?"

I hosted a little Business 101 seminar in prison. Five executives joined me. I had no idea what I was getting myself into, and I'm glad I didn't.

Fifty incarcerated men showed up, and I gave them my best sales pitch: "Instead of selling drugs, what would happen if you used your entrepreneurial skills to start something as simple as a landscaping company? You don't personally need to mow lawns; hire your buddies who are less brave to do the dirty work. And for the first time in your life, you won't have another prison sentence hanging over your head—or have your life on the line, like it was every day when you sold drugs."

Three months later, I was planning PEP's first-ever Business Pitch Competition. I was working hard to recruit executives to fly in and judge the pitches.

I'll never forget the response I got from someone who was known as a "prison ministry veteran" and who had 20 years' experience working in prison. He told me I was out of my mind. "These guys aren't even capable of writing home to their mamas; you think they can write business plans?"

In September, just four months after we began, we hosted the competition. We had 15 CEOs and investors as our judges. One, a member of a billionaire family, flew in from Spain on a private jet. *The Wall Street Journal* even came and wrote about the event.

Now that I'd found my Generous Hustle, I knew I had to leave my real job. Instead of helping rich people get richer, I was committed to working with people on the fringes to build something that mattered. It was going to take everything I had to pull this off.

At the time, I was the Director of Investment Development at American Securities Capital Partners in New York City. I had been flying to Texas monthly to prepare my guys for their big competition, and it was time to stop splitting my time, energy, and focus.

When I quit my job, nearly everyone—my parents, friends, and advisors—thought I had lost my mind. They said I had the potential to do so much more than "just work with inmates."

———

I never thought I'd live in Texas. I didn't want to live in Texas. But despite how crazy others thought I was, I knew this work was my calling. There was no stopping me now. It was 2004: Texas, here I come!

Running PEP's early work remotely was costing me a fortune. Hosting the first competition alone cost me more than $10,000. I had $50,000 in my savings account. By the time I moved to Texas, I had drained my bank account, putting it all into PEP. When I ran out of funds and still didn't have anyone to believe in me, I cashed out my 401(k) and took the early-hit penalty. The guys in prison mattered more to me than my retirement.

I moved to Texas in an old, beat-up minivan. I didn't know where I was going to live, so I stayed at a new volunteer's house. The night I arrived in Houston, I was too exhausted to unpack my minivan.

I woke up the next morning only to see the shattered glass of the car windows. All of my stuff had been stolen. Not only had I drained my bank account down to the last $300, but now I didn't even have clothes to wear.

Some nice people brought me to a small church that morning. Being the only white girl there was enough for me to stand out, but the fact that I was helplessly bawling my eyes out must have led people to wonder what was wrong with me.

I wondered the same thing. What was wrong with me? Leaving an awesome private equity job, moving to Texas, working in prisons, going broke—were my friends and family right?

The church folks found out what had happened to me, and the hundred or so members passed a collection plate. I was handed an envelope containing just over $200. Mostly in ones and fives.

I couldn't believe it. I had gone from having $50,000 in the bank to receiving $200 in charity from people who didn't have much at all. What had I done with my life?

When I told a family member what had happened, he said, "That's what you get for working in prisons. It's probably your own guys who robbed you."

That must have been it. My guys busted out of prison overnight and robbed me.

The more PEP took off in Texas, the more people wanted to put me on a pedestal. That's how I became known as a "prison angel." I was called a "saint who ministered to the Dark Side" and other freaky titles.

I hated the pedestal; my own image felt so fraudulent and unattainable. But when the press called me an angel, what was I supposed to say? "Actually, let me give you a rundown of my faults and mistakes"?

I hadn't lied to create my image, but it felt like a trap. I was so scared for the day that the human me would be discovered. I thought that if

I ever got real with anyone, I'd be a huge disappointment. I was sup-posed to inspire people with my strength and courage. That's what leaders do, right?

Not tell them how deeply I was struggling every day. With every-thing. I didn't know if PEP would work; we experienced failures on some level every day. I had been married since age 22, and I was lost in my marriage. My husband had moved to Texas shortly after I did, and we worked together at PEP for a period of time. Yet when we hit speed bumps, instead of slowing down, I sped up.

The pressure to be perfect kept mounting. To keep up with their an-gel expectations, when people asked me how I was doing, I said I was "blessed." "Happy." "Fine."

The more fake I got, the more my heart needed to burst because of all the pain I was holding in. My fakeness was oozing out of me and it caused me to disrespect myself a little more each day.

Fast-forward a few years: PEP was on a roll. We had an astonish-ing 5 percent recidivism rate, had a 98 percent employment rate, and had recruited 7,500 volunteers, including many top CEOs and MBAs from 32 schools. We had graduated 600 men and served their families as well.

Even though we were teaching entrepreneurship, it was our character development work that was transforming our guys' futures and lead-ing them to real careers.

It's worth repeating: 95 percent of our participants didn't go back to prison. Almost every single one of them got a job. Lives were being changed.

My story and our participants' stories were featured in national news outlets on a regular basis. I was in my twenties and became a face for prison rehabilitation. I was speaking in front of audiences of up to 25,000 people.

By 2008, I had been married for nine years. We were living in Texas, and after a few years of working together, my husband went back to practicing law. I lived much of my life on the road (and in prisons).

My divorce came quickly and unexpectedly. My husband served me divorce papers. I never got to say goodbye.

I should have seen it coming, but I didn't. I was so absorbed in PEP's mission that I had missed many opportunities to be a wife.

The shock, the abandonment, and the shame struck me in a way that I couldn't have prepared for. I was immersed in a Christian community where people believed that "divorce is sin" and "God hates divorce." I had sworn that one thing I would never be in my life was a divorced woman. And now, here I was. PEP was working, but my life wasn't.

I was already condemning myself and feared condemnation from others. So I didn't exactly send a press release about my divorce; I hid in my shame.

I had prided myself on being a tough girl all my life, but now I really needed help. Right after the divorce, I got sick with back-to-back pneumonias. I was hospitalized. Being so ashamed that I couldn't think of anyone to call when I was hospitalized was one of the most pathetic, lonely times I'd ever had. The thought of moving out of my house and throwing away all the pictures of my husband and me felt unbearable.

So I turned to the few people I knew wouldn't judge me: released graduates from PEP, who understood loss, shame, and failure. I turned to them for support at a time when I had no strength. They helped me move out of my house and became my closest confidantes.

During this turbulent time, I made choices that I've regretted to this day. I lost sight of my boundaries and ended up having intimate relationships with more than one graduate.

I hadn't broken laws. The men had been released from prison. But that didn't stop the Texas Department of Criminal Justice (TDCJ) from determining that my choices were inappropriate. Still filled with shame, I didn't disagree with them.

Within a month, TDCJ banned me from all Texas prisons.

I hated my guts.

I thought I could at least stay on with PEP as a fundraiser and advocate, without visiting prisons. Turns out I couldn't. TDCJ said that if I stayed affiliated with PEP, they would shut down the program altogether.

I had some choices about how to disclose my scandal to our supporters. More than anything, I wanted to disappear quietly— or at most, write a letter saying that I was resigning for "personal reasons" and leave it at that.

I was advised that a vague letter coming from the passionate founder would create rumors, not just about me but about PEP, too. For the sake of the organization moving forward, I realized it would be best for me to disclose my mistakes.

So I did it. I prepared a letter to email to PEP's 7,500 supporters, telling them not only about my divorce, but also about my relationships.

Years later, it's still hard to explain the thickness of the shame that swallowed me. I was six feet under this avalanche of self-hate, hardly breathing, wishing I wasn't.

Hitting the Send button on my resignation email was the scariest thing I've ever done in my life. But the day before I sent it, I made another choice. I called the news to snitch on myself.

Throughout my resignation period, I had a fantastic crisis-PR advisor named Angela Dailey. She told me that I was fooling myself if I thought my resignation letter wouldn't end up in the hands of reporters. And she said that reporters would likely have a field day with it. Three weeks before my resignation, the *Dallas Morning News* had written a Sunday morning, front-page article about my success with PEP. Angela advised me to proactively call the *Dallas Morning News* to tell the reporter about the letter I was about to send and give her the choice to break the story.

Right before—and right after—the call, I wanted to take my life. The biggest newspaper in Dallas now had a juicy story of scandal, a come-uppance for a young wannabe, a told-you-so about prison reform. It was a perfect storm of shame.

The reason I called that reporter, out of all the reporters I knew? I could tell she really cared about PEP. I pleaded with her to break my story in a way that would allow PEP's good work to carry on (which it has).

But like a game of telephone, as the story made its way from one news outlet to another and went national, it became sensationalized as a "prison sex scandal" (even though nothing ever happened in prison). Before the story broke in the news, I sent my disclosure email to our supporters.

I was sure I had ruined God's calling for my life.

I had lost my identity as a leader. And as a wife.

I was dead broke.

I really didn't have a reason to live anymore.

———

Maybe 15 minutes after I sent my resignation email, my inbox filled up. I braced myself, anticipating hate mail telling me I was a disgusting human being.

Instead, my inbox filled with nearly a thousand messages of the same love, support, and grace I had preached over the past five years.

We all make mistakes.

We love you.

Thank you for your honesty.

We stand with you.

What are you doing next?

I had no idea about "next."

———

Even before my scandal, my self-hate was choking me. I just couldn't stand being me anymore. I couldn't hear one more person tell me that I was "amazing." They knew the stage me, the crowd-pleasing me.

I knew the real me. The fraud in me ruined any chance of joy.

I decided it was time to come out of the closet. If people came to know the real me and chose to spit on me, that would be what I deserved, what I expected. With nothing to lose, and with the smallest flicker of hope left, I wrote it up—the Last Five Percent. The five percent I had kept hidden, the five percent that was the secret me.

I was a mental slave to this Five Percent and beat myself up relentlessly over it every day. My dirtiest dirt—I packed it down, never shared it with anyone, and prayed that it would never surface. I couldn't believe how it ruled my heart and my life. The Last Five Percent told me that I was not good enough. That I was unacceptable, dirty, disgusting. A failure.

I pulled up a fresh Word document, and the first thing I did was password-protect it. Then I verbally vomited all over it, documenting the most shameful things in my past. The things I had never told my therapist. The things I told myself I had forgotten.

By the time I was done with the seven pages, describing my worst decisions and the worst things that had happened to me, in detail, I felt so vulnerable. Exposed.

And relieved.

Finally, I had decided to be honest with myself.

————

When I screw up, how do I know who to confess it to? Do I just tell the person I hurt? Or to truly feel 'clean,' do I have to tell the world?

A general rule of thumb is: *keep the circle of the confession to the circle of the sin.* Words of wisdom from one of my most trusted advisors.

I had once seen a husband publicly confess his affair to his wife—in front of 40 other people. He broke down telling her and then, in front of all of us, asked her for forgiveness. I'll never forget the embarrassment on her face. She buried her head in her hands and sobbed. *This* was how she had to learn about his affairs?

When she wouldn't readily forgive him, he pleaded, "Please, please, we both believe in forgiveness. I am so sorry. Please forgive me!" He got down on one knee in a dramatic gesture and held her hand.

I was so mad for her. Not only had he betrayed her, but now he was peer-pressuring her for forgiveness. She probably feared looking like a jerk if she stayed stuck at no.

Yes, I forgive you.

Nothing felt right about it.

Keep the circle of the confession to the circle of the sin.

———

I knew that if I didn't send my Last Five Percent out right away, while I was feeling desperately courageous, I would never share it. I made a list of seven people to send it to. Most were my closest friends, but one was a prominent pastor, someone for whom I had the highest respect.

"I'm about to send you a detailed account of the worst things I've ever done. Will you read it?"

He knew how deeply I was struggling with my identity.

Send it.

So I attached the document to an email message and sent it to the person whose judgment I feared the most.

Sometimes I wonder why I started with this pastor. Maybe it was my Catholic upbringing and I wanted a confession and a penance. I wanted him to give me some lashes so I could get what I deserved.

It would have been a lot easier to send it to a fellow screw-up. Had I sent it to someone who had been known for doing worse things than me, I could have easily found grace.

But I wanted to try my hand with the most respectable of them all because what I wanted more than anything—more than lashes—was his blessing and acceptance. I figured that if he could see the Last Five Percent and accept me, maybe I could accept the whole package, too.

———

I anticipated one of two responses:

1. He would be so disappointed in me that he wouldn't respond. It would be the end of our relationship.

2. He would lash me and confirm how messed up I was and, at best, would tell me how much fixing I needed.

The problem with the possibility of either of these responses was that I was one ounce of hope away from being hopeless and taking my life. I was willing to play with fire.

I sent the email.

———

The longest 30 minutes of shame ticked by. I cried for all of it—the self-hate, the self-doubt, stabbing me.

Regrets. Why did I send it to him, of all people?

And then his name popped into my inbox. His response: "That's child's play. That's what the cross is for."

That was it. I wrote seven pages of the most shameful things in my past. He responded with nine words.

My first thought: He clearly didn't read what I wrote. My dirt is not child's play!

My next thoughts: Where is your judgment? Where is my punishment? Tell me how rotten I am!

His response felt so inconsequential—like this pastor was laughing about my past. Did he get it?

I started crying so hard I was shaking. All of my biggest fears about the consequences of coming clean had turned out to be nothing but a story I'd been telling myself.

I read his nine words about 90 times. So simple they were paralyzing.

I shot back to him: "What do you mean, child's play? Did you read what I sent you??"

And he responded: "I want you to pretend that you're floating in a boat in an ocean. My prayer for you is that big gentle waves of grace would wash over you, washing you clean of your shame."

Another mentor had prayed a similar vision for me: "I have a vision of you surrounded from head to toe by an extra-thick wall of shame. I pray that grace will melt this wall of shame off of your body … and that the shame will drip off until all of it forms a puddle under your feet."

I envisioned the waves of grace washing over my body. Washing me clean. The meaning of my name, Catherine, is "pure one." How I longed to feel pure.

I cried more, feeling the tranquility. And for the first time in my life, I felt known, safe, accepted, and loved.

Maybe I was loveable after all.

This isn't a religious or conversion manifesto. However, it would be next to impossible, and disingenuous, to leave my faith out of my journey. My love of grace has only deepened as I've received it—and I believe God was the first to forgive me and to love me for me.

What I understand of Jesus's life strikes me as awesome, but I often struggle with the label "Christian." It has acquired so much political and organizational baggage. I work hard to separate myself from the negativity and division that results from conflicting religious doctrines. I experience God as love. As being for me even when I am against me. I experience unconditional love—and because I receive it, I am able to love others better.

When I was 25, I devoted my life to God and haven't looked back. My faith changed my hustle, my wallet, my priorities, my heart, and my understanding of grace and love.

If it weren't for Christians, I wouldn't be doing this work. My first prison visit in Texas was with Chuck Colson, the founder of Prison Fellowship, a Christian organization. I visited death row with Chuck.

After my resignation from PEP, the first people to show me love were devoted Christians. Some serious pastors reached out with nothing but grace and love for the girl with the sex scandal. Some of my hope for Christianity was restored by the way I was treated when I was a leper to others.

So as I share my journey, you'll see some spiritual stuff. If you're an atheist, take a deep breath. Don't write me off quite yet. We can make a deal—I won't push any religious beliefs on you. Please just don't discount me for being spiritual. I hope you want to hear from the authentic me and not from the edited version of me. My love for God, my neighbor (you), and humanity drives me.

Above all things, my life goal is to live a life of love and service.

————

Feeling a surge of courage from this pastor's acceptance, I tested out this grace thing. Maybe his response was a one-off fluke?

I teed up emails with the Last Five Percent and sent them to the six other closest people in my life. I had no need for the whole world to read my Last Five Percent, but I wanted these six people to know the real me if they were going to be companions on my journey.

Six for six wrote back with love and encouragement. They told me I was brave for my vulnerability. They also told me I didn't have to share my dirt to be lovable.

They were right—I had no obligation to share every part of myself to be worthy of friendship. I had to do it for myself, not for them. I needed to know that the whole me, even the previously hidden me, was suitable for their love and friendship.

Their unconditional love for me finally started to soften this hard-head. I started a new journey, with new beliefs:

I am lovable, accepted, beautiful, forgiven.

I am me. I am human. I am enough. I am no longer hiding.

I am free.

I forgive me.

I love me.

I've never sent the document to anyone since, and have never again felt a need to. That's because I have actually forgiven myself at this point. Compare that to the time before my resignation, when my lack of forgiveness caused me to live every day in my past—in mental torture.

Eight years later, when I think back to the things I included in the Last Five Percent, some seem so stupid and insignificant that I can't believe I ever gave them valuable headspace. I was so judgmental of myself.

And yes, right now I'm judging how judgmental I used to be of myself.

The upside to my public resignation? No one thinks I'm perfect anymore. No one has thought of me as an angel since then. That's not a license to screw up more. It's just some serious freedom from the bars of perfection.

After my resignation, for the first time, I felt loved just for being plain old me. Without my CEO status, I had no results to produce. I was amazed to learn that people cared about me as a human, not just as a leader. That acceptance healed me.

Although I wouldn't wish a public shaming on anyone, there can be something freeing about it. When the whole world knows your mistakes, and your dirt has been spread on the internet, you can also get public healing.

And, I'll forever know who my real friends are and aren't.

The weight of secrecy is a real killer. So many people are dying on the inside, being eaten alive by shame.

Shame thrives in secrecy.

The more secrecy, the more shame.

The more shame, the more we separate ourselves from people who could heal us.

The more separation, the more we hate ourselves.

The more self-hate, the more hopelessness.

The more hopelessness, the more likely we are to self-sabotage.

Again. And again.

A lovely cycle.

———

Within an hour of sending my resignation email, I received my first phone call. It was from Bill Townsend, a serial entrepreneur and investor who lived in Salt Lake City. Bill was a major donor to PEP, but I hardly knew him. I had met him once, briefly, at an airport.

Usually when I met donors, I thanked them profusely for believing in my work, because they were a rare breed. My meeting with Bill was different. He told me to shut up, and he just thanked me for taking on this mission.

He thanked *me!*

Bill's heart of love and grace stretched beyond most humans' understanding. At the airport that day (in our first meeting, before my resignation), we talked about God, forgiveness, redemption, and second chances. Then he made a case that PEP should serve all people, including those who had committed sexual crimes.

I was shocked. Normally, when people (including plenty of Christians) asked me if PEP served people with sexual criminal histories, and I responded that we didn't, they sighed with relief—and they sometimes told me they wouldn't support me if we did. That always made me think, "Huh? You want these guys reentering society as your neighbors, *without* rehabilitation?"

I told Bill that I had asked the Texas Department of Criminal Justice if we could serve people with sexual criminal histories, but they wouldn't allow it. Bill is my kind of guy, the kind who asks "why not?" and "how?" He said, "Let's start a separate organization and program to serve the most stigmatized." I didn't really do anything with his idea, but I didn't stop thinking about it.

When Bill called after my resignation, I was in the most broken state of my life, hardly able to get a word out. He said to me, "Sweetie, we love you. There is nothing you could do to change our love for you. Come stay with my wife Andrea and me for a while. We will love you back to life."

Who were these crazy people? I had nothing to offer them, yet they were just loving me for no reason. What was the motive? I hardly knew Bill, and he was inviting me, the scandalous divorced woman, into his home.

I just simply couldn't believe it.

So I said yes.

I spent the next year in intensive therapy and screw-up camps for leaders.

Apparently, I'm not the only leader to have screwed up. There were plenty of other pastors and CEOs who had never taken time to look inside until they, too, combusted.

I was in a deep depression. Without a vision, a purpose, or passion, I felt lifeless. It was the most quiet, sad, lonely, boring, hard year of my life. Not knowing if I would ever bounce back was the hardest part. I doubted everything.

As I endured that year, I made a promise to God: "All I see is the darkness. I don't see a way to the other side of this, ever. But if you get me through this, I promise I will live to serve you the best I can for the rest of my life, and I promise that if there's any redemption story with my own life, I will use everything I have to create second chances for others."

I had to get my own fresh start. After nearly a year of bouncing around, feeling terrified of making another bad decision, I finally moved back to New York City because it was my favorite city in the world, and I needed some energy back in my bones. I took out a three-month sublease as I cautiously figured out my next steps.

I got an offer to go back into venture capital. I needed that offer to know that I had choices. But the minute I got it, I felt like a complete sell-out. I have known very clearly, since starting PEP, why God put me on earth.

I would flash back to my days in prison—to those graduation ceremonies—and it was only those memories that made me want to keep living.

I founded Defy Ventures in 2010, after one long year of therapy, life boot-camps, and soul-searching.

I sat there frozen in front of my email once again, this time with the Defy announcement ready to go out. I felt nearly as chicken as I had about sending my resignation announcement. What would people think and say about me? "Here she goes again ..."

I could have been permanently paralyzed by my fear. It felt suffocating at times for sure, and I nearly gave in. But in the end, I realized that it was my own judgments of my screw-ups that were my biggest enemy.

As I was dreaming up Defy, one of my mentors told me, "You did PEP in Texas statewide. You have it in you to do this nationally. America needs this. Go big or go home." I thought he was crazy, but I've always liked crazy.

Why not?

Another pastor, who is a good friend and mentor to me, told me, "Defy will be global. The world needs this."

That all sounded nice, and I was glad other people believed in me. But I didn't know how I would even raise my first year's budget on the heels of a scandal. These national and global prophecies seemed totally intimidating.

And outrageously exciting.

At Defy's three-year mark, we had graduated close to 400 men and women. By the four-year-mark, Defy had become a national organization, serving small numbers of released men and women in 11 states.

By now, in year seven, we've served 3,600 men, women, and even youth. We're operating in 19 prisons, including a juvenile prison, in five states, and launching more year after year. We've grown from having 12 staff members, just 18 months ago, to having 55 in 2017.

As of 2017, Defy Ventures is even a bit global-ish. Because of partnering with an amazing entrepreneur named Vicki Wambura, we now have Defy graduates in Kenyan prisons, and some Brazilian prisons are hoping to adopt our work.

When I met women in Brazilian prisons (who are incarcerated with their babies until the children turn six) they pleaded, "Please don't forget about us." I haven't. For now, though, I'm focusing Defy's efforts on disciplined expansion in the U.S., with the goal of starting programs in three to four new states per year.

The U.S. leads the world in mass incarceration (with only 5 percent of the world's population, we have 22 percent of the world's incarcerated population), and we fail miserably at rehabilitation, with a recidivism rate of 76.6 percent. The cost to taxpayers is stupid. In 2017, Californians pay more than $75,000 to incarcerate one person for just one year. By comparison, Defy costs $500 to $2,000 per person per year, and more than 95 percent of our grads keep their freedom.

"The only thing I can't understand is why Defy isn't in every prison in America!" exclaimed a volunteer at a recent prison event.

It's all about the money. And about whether you believe in second chances enough to provide scholarships.

Oh, and it's about the mentality of prison officials. People who are smart about crime understand that without rehabilitation, we aren't creating public safety. After all, prison is called "Corrections," but so often it's just plain punishment.

More and more correctional officials understand that rehabilitation is key. After all, they are public servants entrusted with creating public safety, and more than 90 percent of incarcerated people get out of prison eventually. The California Department of Corrections and Rehabilitation's saying is, "Today's inmate is tomorrow's neighbor."

Warden Clark Ducart of Pelican Bay is one of my favorite human beings. He was trying to get Defy to Pelican Bay for a full year before I finally showed up at his super-remote super-max prison.

Warden Ducart said, "I've never seen anything like Defy, and I've been in corrections for 31 years. One of our SHU graduates told me that Defy opened up the world to him. He believes he can do something other than be a criminal now and that he can focus his energy on something positive rather than going back to his old life. Our men in the SHU need programs like Defy the most. Something has to break the chain to show them there is a different way."

Or consider Warden Dave Long. He wrote, "The short-term benefit of bringing Defy to a prison is reduced violence ... It's not only the current EITs who stay out of trouble; the other inmates who want to get into Defy also start to stay out of trouble." I would have cried when Warden Long announced his retirement, but instead, I offered him a job, and he came right back out of retirement to help further this work. Now he sells other wardens on the value of Defy.

As of 2017, we have five former corrections officials on our staff. And I'm proud that a quarter of our staff is made up of formerly incarcerated people. At Defy, we bring former enemies together to create deep cultural change. In fact, Warden Dave hired Ping Lieu, one of the amazing leaders who did time at his facility. Today, Dave and Ping work in partnership to create second chances.

I recently got an email from Roy, an executive who had just returned from his second prison event: "When I walked into the prison and learned you weren't going to be there, I was disappointed. I hope this next part doesn't offend you—but something happened that I thought was impossible. Danielle led the event, and it was just as amazing as when you led it."

In April 2017, I turned 40. I had won lottery tickets to see *Hamilton*, the Broadway play, for my actual birthday weekend. But I chose to spend that weekend at Pelican Bay instead. I couldn't think of a better tactic to attract volunteers: "If you really love me, you'll be at my prison birthday party—and provide business coaching to our EITs."

In the six months before hitting the big 4-0, I was intensely focused on two things:

1. Evaluating my first 40 years to see what else I could learn from the choices I had made and the impact I had had.

2. Making a plan for my next 40 years.

Just like I have EITs write out their eulogies, I scripted a life well lived for myself.

Here goes:

In 2018, Defy is rolling out a correspondence program that holds the promise to serve any incarcerated person in any prison or jail cell. I'm pumped.

By age 53, I'm pathologically optimistic enough to believe that Defy could serve in every major prison in the United States and serve in every major post-release city. This plan relies on our ability to raise the funds and train an incredible number of underdog-loving leaders.

At age 93, I'm a little old hunchback with a cane who's still getting in these guys' precious faces, pounding messages of self-confidence into their brains.

So Roy's email was the opposite of offensive. I felt fulfilled because it showed me that this vision is scalable and sustainable and much bigger than me. Strong leaders are joining our ranks as volunteers and staff, and they are funding and building Defy chapters in their states.

There will always be crime and incarceration in our country. But I believe that Defy will be a key part of ending the epidemic of mass incarceration and recidivism. I would love to one day put us out of business by solving the problem of mass incarceration.

I see millions of Cosses in our future.

I see kids growing up with moms and dads who tuck them in at night and tell them they love them. I see families who live in freedom—physical, emotional, and financial freedom. I see kids with new legacies: taking over the *legit* family businesses. I see a country where we aren't permanently known for the worst things we've done, but are known for who we are today.

I've not only had a second chance at being a leader. I also have my second chance at being a wife—something I professed I never wanted to be again. The truth is that I was just terrified of failing.

It took the charm of a giant Southern gentleman named Charles Hoke to change my mind. He had played football for Alabama, and it was easy for him to catch my attention when we met on a grungy dance floor in an old Irish pub in New York City in 2012. We married in 2013 and had a very Defy-style wedding: We hired about 20 of Defy's EITs to provide everything from the catering to the decorations.

When I met Charles, he was a bond trader on Wall Street. He quickly became Defy's top volunteer, and a year after we were married, he couldn't resist it any longer: He jumped off the corporate ship, too, to pursue his Generous Hustle.

Today, we build Defy together. It's not the easiest of paths, but it works, and I love doing this work with my partner. I've never wanted kids, but we call Defy our family. We are honored to dedicate our time, finances, and everything into this awesome family of second-chance entrepreneurs.

In my recovery period post-scandal, I could never in a million years have predicted the beautiful outcome of my life today. I used to have this recurring dream that I snuck back into prison in a costume and then got caught and thrown out of prison. I would wake up crying, hating myself all over again.

Yes, I'm an odd one. Prison is my favorite place in the world, because I experience miracles there every day as people begin to have hope and feel human again.

I'm not alone in my passion. Read the blogs of our thousands of volunteers to find out why they feel so alive when they come to prison (www.defyventures.org). Or better yet, sign up online to come to prison yourself. Don't worry; you'll get a visitors' badge, and as long as you don't lose it, you won't get assigned a bunk.

I'm ready to let you in on the second-chance wisdom that others have shared with me, the wisdom that makes me the leader I am today. I'm giving you 100 percent in these coming chapters—my heart and soul are in these pages.

Will you give 100 percent? You won't get a second chance unless you're committed to your journey. I need you to be brave so we can find the beauty that lies just on the other side of the pain.

Ready to generously hustle together?

Let's go!

GRADUATION AND BEYOND

To see and feel the love from strangers changed my whole life. I haven't shed a tear in 35 years. I'm 47 now; I cried like a baby at Defy's Shark Tank competition. In that moment, I knew I belonged to the Human Family.

—Timothy

Warden Ducart wanted Defy in the Pelican Bay SHU because his men needed a reason to transform. Hope is a cure for violence. People stop stabbing each other when they actually believe they can have a positive, legal future.

When the men in the SHU change their behavior, Warden Ducart can get them out of the SHU and back to the regular maximum-security yard, where they will have human contact again.

The current standard: When people in the SHU finish their prison terms, they're released directly from the SHU to the streets. Some people think I'm exaggerating when I say this: literally, from the SHU directly to the streets. Imagine your new neighbors. They're classified as too dangerous for a maximum-security-prison yard, but they return to our communities—most often with zero rehabilitation.

Warden Ducart isn't short on innovation. He created three Defy SHU dorms. He allowed the EITs to move into new SHUs located in the same housing unit, and he provided screens so the EITs could watch Defy video courses (we're on channel 29, with Defy courses running on loop 24-7!). The men can't see one another (because they all face the same wall) but they can shout through their steel doors. That's how they conduct their intense daily Defy peer group activities and assignments. I get reports from Pelican Bay staff that the EITs talk about Defy all day, every day (an advantage of being the only show in town). Only Defy EITs live in these housing units, meaning the men are spared the negative pressures of the gang life, and are immersed in a community of support. They're defying the odds, even in solitary confinement.

It's 2017, and we are preparing to graduate our first SHU cohort at Pelican Bay.

Warden Ducart is so proud of his SHU guys for getting to the Defy finish line that he wants them to have a proper cap-and-gown graduation. He takes a risk: he lets them out of their SHUs for the day. Our grads are shackled in waist restraints and handcuffs, and they are about to enter the same "SHU patio" together. These guys were gang rivals and enemies until they went through Defy. They call themselves brothers now.

They are even allowed their first hugs at graduation, and it's almost like the shackles and waist restraints melted off. They embrace like I haven't seen men do before. Across race lines and across gang affiliations.

They're crazy proud of themselves.

"Pomp and Circumstance" blares. Our executives are on their feet, jumping up and down, cheering at the top of their lungs, clapping as hard as they can. You would think their own sons were graduating today.

Then, one by one, each escorted by two officers, our beautifully robed graduates enter. Normally when they're escorted somewhere, they hang their heads in shame as they walk. This time their heads are held high, so high. Ear-to-ear smiles. I-did-this faces.

The sky is a majestic blue. The sun is shining in full glory. The EITs look up at it. It's their first time seeing the sky, without bars blocking it, in years.

I boo-hoo cry happy tears. I am so damn proud of everything we've accomplished. We, meaning: our extraordinary EITs, our dedicated Defy staff, the brave executives, and the Pelican Bay staff that cares even when they don't have to.

On the stage, the EITs passionately deliver their Shark Tank pitches into the microphone I'm holding for them. (Turns out, holding a mic up to your mouth while you're shackled is challenging.) Not one guy chokes.

Standing ovations like you've never seen.

I wasn't sure how this would work, but the EITs didn't want their shackles to hold them back. So just like at our regular graduation events, the graduates are on the stage together, facing the audience. They reach out and grab one another's hands, like tough guys love to do in prison. They all squat down low.

"When I count backward from three, you're going to go crazy for our grads! Now guys, don't hurt yourselves, but if you want to jump and catch some air ... Three! Two! One! Make noise for Defy's first ever graduating class in the Pelican Bay SHU!"

They actually catch air. Their hands are joined. Their arms are raised like the champions that they are. It's the most amazing thing I've ever seen. I still cry, just writing about it.

The crowd of executives goes nuts. Again.

If we can do it here, we can do it anywhere.

Mike wins the pitch competition. He nails it. And he delivers it in front of a member of the audience who is particularly proud and glowing.

Eden was nine years old when her daddy went to prison. She's 19 now and is in college while working two jobs. It's a challenge for her to get the funds together and make the six-hour haul to Pelican Bay. On the rare occasions when she visited, she had to sit in the booth with four inches of glass between her and her dad and speak into a telephone that didn't work very well.

I call Mike to the stage. He has his prize possession in his hands. It's an adorable teddy bear, customized with a teddy bear T-shirt that he decorated in the SHU yesterday. He also has a rose.

"Eden, your dad has been talking my ear off about you. We're honored you made the trip. Join him on the stage. Your daddy has a gift for you."

Being there for my dad's graduation was the best day of my life. I am so proud of him. Getting to hug him for the first time was everything to me. When I got to take that bear home, I felt like I got to walk out with a piece of my dad.

—Eden

Before graduations, we teach our graduates how to do a proper dance, like a waltz, so they can spin their mothers, children, or partners. Mike's shackles didn't allow him to spin Eden. But that didn't stop him from holding her and swaying as they danced under the sky to Joe Crocker's "You Are So Beautiful."

Maybe now you're starting to get why I live for this stuff.

———

Eden confirmed that she would share her life-giving experience and new hope with the concerned moms, dads, grandmas, partners, and kids of other incarcerated EITs on our conference call. Sixty family members eagerly awaited her on the line. It was one of our regularly-scheduled calls for Defy's Friends & Family program, led by formerly incarcerated Defy staff. The call is designed to encourage our EITs' loved ones. Our Friends & Family program also provides resources, online courses, fun events for our DefyKids (bowling nights, museum tours, etc.), holiday gifts, and access to the graduation events.

Eden never called in.

> *I'm so sorry I didn't make the call last night. I live in
> Santa Rosa, and my house burned down last night in the
> California wild fires. We were given minutes' notice to
> evacuate. I lost everything. I am homeless now.*

Eden called our Family Liaison to share the news.

As I learned this, I'm heading to speak at Slack, the technology company. I tell them Eden's story and about last night's tragedy. The head of Slack For Good is there.

> *We were just looking for a way to help with the wild fires.
> Have Eden make a list of everything she needs replaced.
> We'll provide it.*

Miracles. Every day.

———

I received this letter from Charles:

> *When I came into the prison system on a murder charge,*
> *I was at rock bottom. I had destroyed all the relationships*
> *with my entire family, and finally believed what my dad*
> *had instilled in me through ten years of abuse—that I was*
> *no good and would never amount to anything. I was certain*
> *that the rest of my life would be spent behind fences.*
>
> *Why bother trying to improve? Why try changing and*
> *overcoming the obstacles that I had placed in my life? Who*
> *cared and where would it take me anyway?*
>
> *I lost my vision when I went into the Marine Corps in 1972,*
> *and it didn't come back until another inmate, my mentor,*
> *had me enroll in Defy's CEO of Your New Life program, in*
> *which I became an Entrepreneur-in-Training.*
>
> *On Dec. 17, 2015, I won third place in the inaugural Defy*
> *Pitch Competition here at California State Prison Solano. I*
> *got my life back that day. It was the happiest and best day of*
> *my life. I finally have become the person I wanted to become.*
> *I finally solidified the direction I wanted to go in in life. I*
> *finally felt and gained the acceptance I've been looking for. I*
> *found out that this toothless old man has value and is ready*
> *to return to society.*
>
> *Investors informed me that my idea was realistic, valued,*
> *and needed. Others advised me to seek Defy once I paroled,*
> *and they'd back me. My vision is to open Royalty Drain*
> *and Sewer Plumbing in Sacramento, El Dorado, and Yuba*
> *Counties, starting with 10 trucks and 30 employees, many of*
> *whom will be other EITs.*

Before that day, I rarely smiled. Today, I smile, I talk, I encourage, I lead. I'm happy and at peace.

—*Charles*

"I'm a second-generation felon." That's how Rob Lilly, who graduated from Defy's first class in New York City, introduced himself to me.

We got to see him transform his drug dealing skills—and identity—as he gained confidence in himself. After Rob's release, he was working for a nonprofit serving young fathers. Through Defy's incubator, he started Powerhouse Catering on the side, as he's always had a passion for cooking. He grew his catering business and has hired more than 20 formerly incarcerated people. He has a passion for good fatherhood, too, so he mostly hires young fathers, ages 18 to 24.

About a year after starting Powerhouse on the side, Rob got to leave his day job to devote his full-time efforts to his catering business. Powerhouse provides gourmet meals that come with an inspiring story.

My husband, Charles, and I had a second-chance wedding, and Rob and his proud second-chance employees catered it. They provide excellence with a whole lot of heart.

Jose wrote me about his experience with his beautiful 14-year-old daughter:

I'm totally Team Defy for life. I hadn't seen my daughter in 13 years, and had it not been for Defy, I still wouldn't have seen her to this day. And there's a chance I would have never seen her, the way things were going.

I wanted to change things, but I didn't know how. Then we hit the chapter on Meaningful Apologies, and it was on! I started writing letter after letter, with all the things I had learned from Defy. Especially to never give up! I was determined.

I told myself no matter what, I'm going to fix things. I'm going to see my daughter, and hold her, and tell her I love her. And it worked.

And now after seeing her, it transformed my life even more. The only thing that matters now is getting home to her and my family. The graduation changed my life, literally.

It's funny how Defy calls it CEO of Your New Life. Because it actually gives us a new life. One that makes us proud. That makes our families proud. A life that we want our legacy to be about.

Oh yeah, and as for those little teddy bears that people think might not be a big deal? I was going to tell the world that they're actually the biggest deal ever. How we get to write those meaningful messages on the teddy bear's t-shirt.

But yeah, my daughter even posted photos on something called Snap Chat (or something like that?). So yeah, it's a big deal. It's the first thing she's gotten from me in pretty much her whole life.

It's funny because the graduation was Saturday, so my family stayed until Sunday, and my parents told me that she never put her bear down. She held her bear on the whole trip home. My mom was telling me it was sort of bittersweet. Happy and sad. Happy that she had a bear, and loved it so much, but sort of sad, how she was so attached to it, because it was the only thing she had as a close connection to me. That's why she cherished it so much.

It means the world to me that the bear means the world to her.

What Defy does—you can't put a price on it. It reunited me with my family and daughter. Dancing with my mom, giving her that rose. It was worth all the money in the world.

For most people this might sound crazy, but I'm not most people. Maybe I am a little crazy, but isn't that what makes me a good entrepreneur? Blame it on the SHU syndrome. ☺

One day my daughter and I will be traveling with Defy, telling the story of how Defy brought us together and changed our lives. Our first hug, our first dance, our first I love you. Our first day of ever feeling complete or alive.

I was going to say that I have two complaints about Defy.

#1. What took you so long to get to us?

#2. Why does it have to be so short? The graduation was the greatest and saddest day. Sad because it was so short. We need that Marathon program!

Warmest regards,

Jose

P.S. We're changing your name from Catherine Hoke to Catherine Hope.

As part of our Friends & Family program, I had approved a $7,500 expense to fund the bus that scooped up families, starting in Los Angeles, and transported them 15 hours *each way* to Pelican Bay and back, and to cover their hotel rooms.

Best $7,500 I've ever spent. I agree with Jose. You can't put a price on it.

———

Imagine being locked up for ten years. Yes, for a bad decision you made. Like the last time you got in your car after drinking just one too many, and you hit someone, and they died.

Society sees you as a dangerous felon. You see yourself as the same parent with the same heart for the same children you loved and raised—before you were separated from them because of your DWI manslaughter charge. Every day, you are tormented by having missed all of your child's firsts. At the holidays, you want to spoil your child like any other parent does. Not only can you not buy gifts, but the four-inch glass wall between you and your family often deters them from visiting in the first place.

I live for the graduations, when the kids run up. Dad scoops his adorable kiddo into his arms.

> *I love you so much, baby. You are everything to me. I can't wait to come home soon. I promise I will never leave you again.*

"How do you feel about your daddy today?" I ask.

> *I love my daddy. I'm proud of my daddy. I want my daddy to come home with me.*

"Amazing Grace" plays, and the EITs pick up red roses to present to their moms, their wives, and the fathers who occasionally show up.

Ross wrote,

> *The graduation ceremony is what not only I, but every EIT prepares for. I was fortunate enough to have my sister and 9-year-old daughter present for this milestone in my life. My daughter, Johanna, was born July 11, 2007. I was sentenced to 12 years in prison one month after her birth.*
>
> *Within my first six months in prison, Johanna's mother had dropped her off at my sister's house. Today, nine years later, my daughter calls my sister mom and calls my sister's husband daddy.*
>
> *On October 5th, 2016, I graduated Defy. I got to present roses to my guests. I gave my sister Vincentia one of them, and kissed her on the forehead. The other rose went to my 9-year-old daughter Johanna.*

Then Ms. Hoke instructed us to pick up our teddy bears for the kids. I whispered into Ms. Hoke's ear my personal circumstance, that Johanna knows me as Ross, not as daddy. Ms. Hoke clearly didn't hear me, because she said to Johanna, Little girl, can you please come up here. Ms. Hoke asked her name, and said, Your daddy has a teddy bear for you—come get it.

I honestly believe that Johanna still didn't know that I was her daddy. But she came to me with open arms, and Ms. Hoke said, Ross, go ahead, give her your 'love bomb.' I began, Baby girl, you are my inspiration and I got you, you feel me?

And she responded to me, I feel you, Daddy.

That brought tears to my eyes, to my daughter's eyes, to Ms. Hoke's eyes, and to the eyes of everyone in the room—every last one of the EITs. Now I know that when I set goals, I am capable of achieving them.

Microsoft gave Shelley an offer. Then they rescinded it.

Shelley Winner graduated from Defy's first program in a women's prison. She served far less time than most grads—only two years, and for a non-violent drug charge. She had followed in the footsteps of her father to prison, and she sobered up after a long fight with drugs.

Though Shelley had never worked in technology, she just knew she loved tech and was dead set on landing a tech job.

Google jump-started Shelley's technology access. They're one of our best corporate partners, donating more than $1 million with 450+ Googlers engaged as volunteers. They generously provide each of our released graduates with a laptop, a Pixel phone, and $300 of airtime. Imagine trying to get a job without these tools.

Shelley says she "won" the best-ever Defy mentor the day she was connected to Deedee after her release. Deedee is a technology executive who cared for Shelley as if she were her own daughter. Deedee helped Shelley navigate the world and even funded a technology-training program for her.

Finishing this tech-training program qualified Shelley for a Microsoft job. She is charismatic and has some mad sales skills.

Some states now have "ban the box," a law that forbids companies from asking job applicants to check a box on their applications if they have criminal records. The law prevents employers from discriminating against people with criminal histories, so long as the crime isn't related to the job (*e.g.*, a former bank robber probably won't be hired as a bank teller). Shelley knew that Microsoft had made a mistake in rescinding the offer because of her drug charge, so she fought it. She got the decision reversed, and they rehired her.

Six months later, Shelley was recognized by Microsoft as a "Most Valuable Player." She's been promoted since, becoming the top revenue generator on her team. She was even flown to Seattle headquarters to celebrate her accomplishments.

More companies have decided that they want to hire more people with criminal histories, all because of the outstanding leadership and role modeling of people like Shelley.

Defy loves fair-chance employers.

It's a good thing that Shelley's a fighter. She's still navigating some challenges. A year and a half after her release, Shelley lives in a halfway house. Despite a solid Microsoft income, she struggles to find a place that will accept her. Just like many employers, many landlords also discriminate against people with criminal pasts. Even if the offenses were minor drug charges. Even if they happened 20 years ago.

Sometimes Shelley's parole officer won't issue her a pass to see her 4-year-old son, Jase. She lives in a county only 30 miles from him. Perhaps the rationale is that letting a "woman like Shelley" travel between counties could be a real threat to society.

One step at a time, I guess.

Speaking of steps, time for *you* to step to the line.

———

WE ALL MESS UP.
(IT'S NOT "IF," IT'S "WHEN.")

I don't know if this statistic is true, but I've heard that people get speeding tickets for only one out of every 400 driving infractions. I know I've gotten away with thousands of infractions, and I've gotten only one ticket (on my way to prison, of all places). I guess I'm ahead of the curve.

America is the land of second chances, but not for everyone. So who gets a second chance, and who doesn't—and what makes the difference?

For incarcerated people who don't have a program like Defy, few get a second chance when they return to their communities. Maybe it's because society is scared of them. Or because some people with criminal histories don't know how to go about getting a second chance. And yes, there are some (a small minority) who don't want a second chance, because they don't think they deserve one.

At Defy, every EIT gets a second chance, and they make the most of it. They make their families and communities believe again.

I'm sure there have been times in your life when you wanted a second chance, and you didn't get one. Is it luck or a lottery? Or are there certain things we choose to do—or fail to do—that predict our futures?

Why is it that some people get a second chance when others don't?

Let's start by talking about the things that make second chances a whole lot harder to land:

- ¶ Lying after screwing up

- ¶ Having no remorse

- ¶ Being apathetic about your mistake

- ¶ Not taking full ownership and responsibility

- ¶ Not being able or willing to show how you've changed and are committed to a better future since you messed up

- ¶ Repeating the same mistakes

- ¶ Not giving yourself a second chance: keeping yourself locked in a mental prison of self-punishment; beating yourself up, so you have self-defeating behaviors and wallow in self-pity

- ¶ Lacking a positive vision for your future; why even try?

I knew a pastor who complained about his "graceless" church when he was kicked out of it after having an affair. But he continued in the affair, kept lying, and didn't take responsibility for the pain he caused his wife and kids.

Maybe you've screwed up so badly that you don't think you deserve a second chance. I get it; I've been there plenty of times. But if we want anyone else to give us a second chance, we better think about taking responsibility for our past, and then giving ourselves a chance first. If we don't believe in ourselves, why would anyone else?

Some of my guys have a hard time accepting Defy—not because they don't want it, but because they feel like they don't deserve this opportunity. Imagine that you were abandoned by your own drug-addicted parents as a child and put into foster care, where those parents abused you. Why would you believe in yourself when even the people who brought you into this world chose drugs over you, and when the people who chose to take you in didn't take care of you?

Maybe you can relate. Why would you believe in yourself when you just got dumped? Or got fired for cause? Or rejected? Or you just screwed up for the hundredth time after swearing you would never do that thing again?

If you are 100 percent convinced that you don't deserve a second chance, or that _____ [insert the name of whoever offended you] doesn't deserve one or is unforgivable, stop reading now. But if even a small part of you wants to keep reading, maybe you're not done yet.

I'm a product of a conjugal visit. My mom met my dad in prison, married him, and got pregnant with me all while he was in prison. Within one year of his release, my dad went back to a life of drugs and crime.

One night, in a jealous, drug-fueled rage, he beat my mom almost to death. It all started with her holding me in her arms. She left the next day and would then try to raise a man by herself. She did her best to provide a good life for me, working two jobs as a waitress. This left me to be raised by the streets.

My first incarceration was at 11 years old. I beat up a 13-year-old kid and was taken to juvenile hall. This was the beginning of group homes and boot camps and other ways the system took me away from the only love I ever knew: my mother's love. So I grew up in the system, angry and bitter towards everyone and everything.

Until Defy, I've never been around people who want to help others. I want to be one of those people now. I have a vision now, and that vision is to make the world a better place. It all started with Defy.

—Justin

Is Defy Justin's second chance? Or is it his legitimate first chance?

Does Justin deserve a chance to start over, even though he committed a violent crime as an 11-year-old?

———

We call this sector criminal *justice*.

We call it the land of liberty and justice *for all*.

Yet my guys are called ex-offenders for life.

———

It's important to recognize the injustice that is so prevalent in our criminal justice system, while also recognizing the injustice you might be self-inflicting—injustice brought on not by law enforcement but by your own guilt and shame.

I'm guessing some of these thoughts will pop into your mind as you read about others' mistakes:

No, my mistake really is different.

Mine is worse.

The reason no one will forgive this mistake is because ___ .

We tend to think that our mistakes are so special or unique that no one else could possibly understand them. I don't know your bad decisions, but I'm guessing they've been made thousands or millions or billions of times before. The worst part of messing up is that it usually causes us to isolate or distance ourselves and rot in our shame, all alone.

As one of my mentors told me, the only way to get to the other side of the pain is to go through it, so let's go.

Warning: It's normal, when we know we're about to dive into pain, to feel tired, to have other priorities surface, to let ourselves get distracted—because escaping pain is always easier in the short term. But with escape comes compounding consequences. I'm guessing that you wouldn't be reading this book if escape were serving you so well.

You have to want to get to the other side of the pain. Be brave. You will make yourself proud if you live this book. You probably can't see it now, but failing can lead to the best things in our lives if we do a good job of learning from our messes.

I tell my guys at a Defy Kickoff, "If you like doing time and crime, get out. You want more of the same old same old? This isn't the place for you. But if you're ready for a second chance, you're ready for Defy because we're going to get real. If you're ready to be the CEO of Your New Life, please stay."

My goal is to make you uncomfortable with these stories of underdog victories. Uncomfortable enough to evolve your thinking about yourself and about second chances. My hope is that you won't just be a spectator in these stories, but will stretch by applying the wisdom to your mess-ups and to those of people in your community.

A few years ago, I spoke to several hundred very wealthy, self-policing, upstanding, conservative religious men at a business conference. They fully lived up to their stereotype: handsome, well-groomed, friendly Boy Scout types. Why they invited a woman with a sex scandal to address their rigid audience was a mystery to me until a few minutes after I took the stage.

I started like I always do:

> *What would it be like if you were known only for the worst thing you've done?*
>
> *Think back to the worst decision you've made, the one you regret the most, the one that caused you or others the most pain. Maybe it was something criminal. Maybe it wasn't. Maybe it was emotionally or morally or spiritually wrong.*
>
> *Maybe it was an act of omission.*
>
> *What labels could people have attached to your mistake?*
>
> *Now, I know you nice-looking overachievers don't look super-naughty, but I'm going out on a limb here, guessing that maybe, long, long ago in your past, there was a time or two ... or three ... when, you know, you ... secretly had a lustful thought (okay, just once!) or something?*

Knowing laughter.

Oh, really? Tell me more?

They laughed more heartily.

It's a funny thing, but my favorite audiences are often the ones that are the most culturally locked up. Those who suffer under the strictest, most graceless of regimes, accountability, and judgment.

Like the time when I spoke to a group of a hundred of the wealthiest little old ladies. They came all glammed up because if they have the wrong outfit or the wrong Botox injection, they're out of the club. They're all about keeping up with the Joneses, and they're stuck behind the bars of perfection.

Or when I've spoken in super-conservative churches. The kind of church that trains you how to answer religiously so that you don't get judged out of the congregation:

How are you?

I'm blessed.

How's your wife?

She's gorgeous and happy.

How's your job?

Couldn't be better.

The kind of church where you have to dress fancy and have your stuff 100 percent together to even be let in. It's also the kind of church where you talk about how you sinned sometime in the past (long ago!), but because of the blood of Jesus, you're now saved and perfect.

At that religious businessmen's conference I mentioned above, you could have heard a pin drop when I told them about my scandal. It's normal for the room to get really quiet during my sad part. But with these guys, it was different. I could *feel* them. I could see their gulps, their own shame on their faces, even though the lights were dimmed over the audience. I could hear their secret shame when they nervously laughed in the wrong places.

And that's why I love speaking to audiences who are the most oppressed by their cultures of judgment. Because then when I turn the corner with my own story of climbing out of my mess, and learning to love myself, and being imperfect but still contributing, they cheer louder for me than anyone else does.

The cheering they are sending my way is the cheer they want for themselves. They see my freedom. They want their freedom.

When I bring an EIT up on stage and he confesses that he killed someone in a drive-by as a teenager, and did 20 flat, and now runs a business and has transformed his entire life, the trapped audiences give him a standing ovation.

Because my EIT is free—not just from physical prison, but from the prison of perfection.

COMING CLEAN

"If you knew the real me, you wouldn't love me or accept me."

I'm hanging out in the classroom with our released men and women (people with criminal histories can start Defy on the outside if they didn't start in prison). After 18 months of hard work, tomorrow is the big day. For finishing Defy, they're about to earn a Baylor University MBA program certificate.

"You've all been through so much. Visualize how proud your families will be tomorrow night! Share how you feel about yourself for defying the odds."

They go around the circle, and with vulnerability, talk about how they wanted to quit a million times and why finishing Defy represents the greatest achievement of their lives.

Until we get to Rolando, a big guy who has always been so composed. His lips are quivering. "It's all a lie!"

"What's a lie, Rolando? You've done this! You've earned this! We're so proud of you." The other EITs comfort him.

Rolando says,

> Tomorrow will be a sad day for me. A day that will remind me what a disappointment I've been all my life.
>
> My wife, parents, and daughter will be there to see me receive my Baylor MBA certificate. This is the biggest

*accomplishment of my life, and my first time in a cap and
gown. But only I will know this, and now you all know this.*

*My family thinks this is no big deal. Because for the last 20
years, I have been living a lie. They all think I graduated
from college and held jobs that I didn't really have. I wanted
them to think I was smart. I wanted to be good enough for
my wife. I started lying young, and I piled one lie on top of
another, and now all of me is a lie. So tomorrow, when I will
have finally finished one honest thing, no one in my family
will know my joy, because they won't understand how
sacred this cap and gown are to me. And I won't have the
real joy because the Rolando they know is a fraud.*

I am so exhausted by my lies. I just want to be free.

It was one of those moments when, as a teacher, I want to have the
perfect solution handy. But I don't. Rolando starts weeping, and so
do we. We can feel his pain and fraud because we all relate to it.

If living a lie is so exhausting, what's our alternative?

————

The girl had ground her rugby cleat into my neck. To say it left a mark
is an understatement. It looked like a hickey gone bad.

At this UC Berkeley rugby match, our rivals didn't play nice. That
was fine on the field, but as a graduating senior, I was preparing for
my biggest career interview, scheduled for two days later. It was for a
venture capital job at Summit Partners, doing technology investing.
I really wanted it.

I couldn't find a turtleneck that would cover up my neck wound.
It was butt-ugly and the first thing anyone noticed about me. I was
embarrassed. So embarrassed.

The interviewer from Summit came out to shake my hand. I stood and shook his, and said, "Look, I know my neck looks really messed up. It's not a hickey, I swear. I play rugby, and a girl stepped on my neck with her cleat. I couldn't find a proper cover-up." We then proceeded with the interview.

I got hired.

Why was I so terrified to tell him about my messed-up-looking neck? Why was I so embarrassed? I don't even know.

So many of my EITs have tattoos—sometimes, offensive tattoos, everywhere. Like on their necks. Some of those tattoos make for a messed-up-looking neck. On top of a messed-up-looking rap sheet.

We can't change our pasts—or our necks. But instead of hiding, we can be forthcoming and take control of the story. We can tell it our way.

What if I had never talked about the rugby field? My interviewer would have pretended not to notice the mark, even though he would have awkwardly glanced at it a dozen times. He would have turned me down, probably judging me as a stupid co-ed with bad judgment who couldn't afford a turtleneck. And of course, I would never have been told the real reason for my rejection.

We fear being honest, but usually, our truth is far less daunting to others than we make it out to be. And it's certainly less daunting than the stories that other people make up about our marks, left unexplained.

Why not control the narrative and tell it on our terms?

———

Confession time turns most of us into chickens.

Think of the worst thing you've done. Now imagine having to tell the world about it. Most of us humans are born with a nature that makes us want to do one of two things after we screw up: (1) Hide it. Or (2) if we realize that we can't hide it and think we might get caught, we want to lie about it, deny it, or minimize it.

Think of a 3-year-old getting busted for stealing cookies out of the jar before dinner. The textbook response, even when caught red-handed: "No, I didn't."

We screw up. Then we lie. It's a human pattern.

What would happen if we screwed up, *but we didn't lie?* How could it change our chance of a second chance, and everything else about our future?

My husband, Charles, is 6'7". The first time I took him skiing, he fell a lot. And six feet is a long way to fall. When Charles's caveman body hits the snow, it hurts because it's so much mass crashing at once.

As a natural extension of my high school wrestling (where I was the first girl on the team—that should explain a lot), I started training in Brazilian jiu-jitsu (BJJ) when I worked in private equity. The first thing you learn in BJJ is how to "break fall." You know you're going to get taken down and thrown, so learning to hit the mat safely is important.

How come most of us are never taught how to "break fall" for life and leadership?

Every leader I've met has done at least one thing in his or her past that is so messed up that if this thing came to light, he or she would have to resign or would at least be in personal crisis.

The farther we rise, the farther we have to fall. The farther we fall, the more it hurts.

It seems that the more we accomplish in life, the greater our need is to bury the skeletons deeper in the closet. Because if they're ever found, they will cost us everything we've spent our entire lives building.

The more we bury, the more we feel like a fraud, like Rolando, and the more we disrespect ourselves. The more we disrespect ourselves, the more likely we are to continue making self-sabotaging decisions.

Shame thrives in secrecy. When I got served divorce papers, I didn't want to tell anyone. Except my graduates—because they knew I was imperfect like them, and they would accept me no matter what.

Quick tips on confession:

1. I always have to confess to myself first before I can confess to anyone else. That might seem obvious. But if I deceive, deny, or minimize my mistake when I tell myself what happened, it's unlikely I will succeed in confessing to anyone else.

2. I've learned to identify safe people for the confession. Sometimes I immediately confess directly to the person I've hurt, but other times I've found it smarter to first confess to someone who wasn't directly affected by my choices and get advice on how to most effectively confess to those I did hurt. Not everyone will love and accept me for who I am when I confess, but I have the discernment to generally know who is a safe person to start with.

3. Confessing first to a therapist can be a great starting place.

4. If I know I will need to come clean with a group, starting with a small subset of more-trusted safe people within that group is easier. I come clean with them—or even just one of them—and then ask them to be in my corner when I come clean with the larger group.

5. I've learned to keep the circle of the confession to the circle of the sin. A public confession and apology, like the ones I gave with my scandal, are rarely needed or appropriate. In that case, I sent my confession to our 7,500 supporters because my actions—and resignation—affected all of them. But that event has been the only outlier in my life; every other confession has been made privately, person to person, or to the group of people I've directly offended or otherwise affected.

6. I've learned to be complete with my confessions so that I'm not lying or minimizing the truth (which could lead me to lose credibility a second time).

7. I've also learned the value of not sharing TMI (too much information). Using my resignation as an example, I shared that I went through a divorce, crossed boundaries, and had relationships. At first when I confessed, I felt obligated to divulge everything to anyone who probed, but I learned how inappropriate it is for people to dig, and how unnecessary (and more hurtful) it can be to share TMI. Now when nosy people try to dig for sensational details, I tell them that it's not their business, thank you very much. Sharing details is often counterproductive. When someone starts digging, before answering the question, ask yourself (and maybe even the person), "Does this person *really* need to know this? If so, why? What is their motive for asking in the first place? If they know the answer, will it truly help or hurt them?"

8. A confession is important. But the apology is what matters when you're in relationship with people. A confession is *not the same* as an apology. Read on.

IMPRISONING LIES

Maintaining our personal prison takes consistent effort and brain-washing. We have to continually dehumanize ourselves and remind ourselves just how shameful we are. After all, if we stop the trash-talking, we might escape our own prisons.

Imagine that!

If my guys, who have committed crimes and been taken from their children, can start to believe in themselves and their futures again, I know you can get there, too.

—————

Why have I either lied or been tempted to lie every time I've screwed up? Because I have this tape playing in my head: "If they know the real me, they won't love me or accept me."

How much of this sounds familiar?

I lie when I think the real me is not good enough. When the real me is unacceptable.

But when I really think about it, is it because "they" can't accept the real me—or because I can't accept the real me?

I've hated the real me so much. The real me has disappointed me again and again. My screw-ups have been intolerable to me. Surely if I can't love or accept the real me, no one else could possibly love or accept me, because I am broken. Inadequate.

Lying to others will be easier if I lie to myself first. If I tell myself the lie enough times, I will believe it. Then I will be able to sell others the lie. Then maybe I will be loved and accepted.

Except …

I will always know my truth.

I will hate myself more for lying to myself and for lying to them.

I am a fraud.

The more of a fraud I am, the more I disrespect myself.

I hate myself.

I can't believe in myself again.

The more I'm down on myself, the more I sabotage my future.

But I don't have a future worth investing in anyway, so who cares?

So I pour more energy into covering my shameful past, to salvage the little bit of myself that is intact (or that people believe exists).

I lie again to cover the lie, and then I lie to cover that lie.

I am an avalanche of lies.

Why is it that I never get to freedom?

Even if I get out of prison, I will live the rest of my life incarcerated in my head and heart.

Because I choose to believe that if you knew the real me, you would not love me or accept me.

And I've tried showing the real me a few times, and look where it led me.

So I choose to believe that no one is safe.

I trust no one.

I hate myself in secret.

———

Want to break out of your prison (your head, I mean)? Who would you become if you replaced these lie cycles with positive statements?

We start Defy sessions together by shouting affirmations. It's corny, but I don't care because it works.

I explain to the EITs that breaking free emotionally requires brainwashing. And then I warn them that I will be washing their brains with clean messages. The EITs are usually a (rightfully) distrustful audience to begin with, so by this point, they're peering at me with skeptical and unforgiving scowls.

Yes, brainwashing. I learned from one of my mentors, Dr. Henry Cloud, that all of our brains get dirty with experience. And unfortunately, we're often incapable of washing that dirt out of our own brains without outside influence.

How do we clean our brains? By allowing someone else to wash our brains with cleaner water. Success requires a lifetime of rinsing.

Affirmations are positive statements that we wash our brains with, even when we don't fully believe them. We don't promise to believe them; we *aspire* to believe them.

The EITs stand up and square off, face-to-face, so close they're up in each other's coffee breath, and yell the affirmations at each other as they repeat after me:

I am a Defy EIT.

I am proud of myself.

I can hold my head high.

People know my past and love me anyway.

I am forgiven.

I choose to forgive me.

I am worthy of the love I am receiving.

I am in a community that believes in me.

I am an entrepreneur.

I am the CEO of My New Life.

I am defying the odds.

I have already won, just by being here today.

I will succeed today.

Succeeding feels good.

I am a proud Defy EIT!

His mouth says, "I can hold my head high," but his head is hung and his eyes are glued to the floor, instead of looking at his partner.

I'm like a hawk. I can spot the one guy out of the hundred in the room who doesn't believe it.

"I don't care if you don't believe it ... YET! You right there! Pick your head up, stare your partner dead in the eyes, and do this right! Your loudest, proudest man voice; nothing less! You can do it! Fake it 'til you make it!!! Repeat after me with all you've got this time: I can hold my head high!"

He picks his head up. But he's usually mad at me for calling him out. One of two things happens from here:

1. He yells out the affirmation because of his anger or embarrassment. And then he finishes the rest of the affirmations in style

   or

2. He mumbles it a second time.

When I get response #2, he gets this: "How are you going to convince anyone that you're worth it if you can't convince yourself first?! How are you going to convince the parole board that they should let you out? I need MORE! How many of you think this guy has more in him?"

The crowd nervously starts yelling to encourage him. Then I yell, "One more time! Give me all you've got! Repeat: I can hold my head high!"

And yes, I usually get a little more out of him.

But it's still pathetic, unconvincing, and not enough. I want to push these guys to the edge, but not over it. I could keep picking on him, but I stop—and keep my eye on him. If his energy rises, which it usually does, then I praise him for the improvement.

"I knew you had it in you! Look what happens when you use your strong voice!"

We resume affirmations as a group. They belt out the affirmations this time, not because they believe them initially, but because they're terrified that I'll single them out, too.

By the time I return for subsequent training sessions, the brainwash penetrates even the most stubborn of minds. I don't need to pick on those guys to get them to hold their heads high. They belt out the affirmations with pure confidence, their shoulders back, their chins up. Dignity is restored. They naturally bear-hug, cheer, and high-five each other at the end of affirmations.

In women's prisons, the sound is so different and so sweet. I'm not as used to the higher pitch of the voices. The women yell the affirmations so loudly that half of them are crying; good crying. Just as real and just as mighty.

———

What parts of your brain could use a power wash?

APOLOGIES AND RESPONSIBILITY

I caught my case 15 years ago.

"Oh, really? You 'caught' it, sort of like catching a cold?"

The EIT gives me a cold look.

Sort of. I was at the wrong place at the wrong time. But I guess it was meant to be. Everything happens for a reason.

"Hmmmm. Let's break that down. Tell me about your crime."

He tells me that he was the getaway driver. He and his partner drove to a rival gang member's house. Their intention was only to rob them (by his words, it was to "take back what was ours").

They had no plans to kill the guy.

Things got out of hand for his partner. The EIT stayed in the car through the altercation. When the partner got to the car, he had blood on his hands.

The partner, who snitched to the police, got 15 years. The EIT, who stayed loyal to street code, got 20 to life and was charged with murder—for being the getaway driver. The accomplice.

He's now served 25 years and has seen the parole board twice. Both times, the board denied him parole. The EIT is mad at the world for this injustice—especially because his so-called partner has already enjoyed ten years of freedom.

"I can see the injustice in this. I can see why you're so mad about still being here. But what if I told you that the way you're framing this story to yourself—and to others, including the parole board—is the main reason you're still in prison? If there was another way to truthfully tell the story, and this way could lead to your freedom, would you want to hear it?"

The EIT gets half-curious.

"The story we tell ourselves about what happened is sometimes more important than what actually happened. You're telling yourself the victim version, which keeps you in the victim's shoes. Even though it's a true version, it keeps you feeling sorry for yourself and mad at the world. If you want to stay in that place, keep telling yourself you 'caught' this case and were in the wrong place at the wrong time.

"But I'll tell you a different true version of the same events. Pretend you're a parole board member hearing this account of the same story:

> *I was living an illegal lifestyle as a lost teenager. My father was in a gang, and I followed in his footsteps into the gang. At the time, I thought I was doing the right thing, but now I see how foolish my criminal lifestyle was.*
>
> *When I was 16, I was finally arrested. It was hard getting sentenced as an adult when I was still a kid and felt the need to physically prove myself because I was smaller than everyone else. But coming to this place might have saved my life. That's grace, and I'm thankful for it.*
>
> *I was charged with murder and given 20 to life. I didn't commit the murder, but I was an accomplice by being at the scene and serving as the getaway driver to my partner who committed the murder. Afterwards, I refused to cooperate with law enforcement, so I received a heavier sentence than my partner, who has already been free for ten years now.*

*Today I realize that I am paying the price for engaging in a
lifestyle, and for keeping company, that led to so much pain
and destruction, and a lost life. Growing up in this place has
been a struggle, but I've used this time to look inside and
reflect. I understand what led up to my criminal choices. I
take full responsibility for my past actions. Today, I spend
my time mentoring other young men in prison. I earned my
GED and my associate's degree. I'm a leader in a violence
prevention group. I have learned patience. I meditate
daily and choose peace. I no longer have a short fuse and
understand the value of delayed gratification.*

*Now, at the 25-year mark, I assure you that I've learned my
lesson. I know you have a difficult choice to make and you're
wondering if I'll honor your choice if you grant me freedom.
I promise you that if you give me a second chance, I will not
only make you proud; I will contribute to society. I have
an employment plan, a mentor, and a community that will
hold me accountable. And my son was a year old when I left
him. We've written all these years, and he wants his father. I
believe it's never too late, so I've taken parenting classes. I'm
ready to be a father to my 26-year-old and make him proud.*

"What do you think your future would look like if you actually believed this statement of taking responsibility, and could communi-
cate it with humility and confidence? How would it change your
heart, your actions, and your chances of making parole?"

I hear "everything happens for a reason" every day. Usually it's code
for "God must have wanted this for me." I spar with EITs over this.
"Oh, really? You think God wanted you to hurt that man? Or for you
to be away from your kids for all these years?"

I actually do believe that most things happen for a reason. Usually
the reason we go to prison is because we were committing crimes, not
because prison is our destiny.

If we don't take responsibility, we can't apologize with sincerity. It's rare that a man will make parole if he cannot take responsibility for his actions and meaningfully apologize for them. But there are so many payoffs for keeping ourselves in the victim's seat.

———

What's stopping you from "making parole" and getting out of your own "prison"?

Are you taking responsibility, or are you more comfortable cruising in the victim's seat?

How can you change the narrative so you get to freedom?

———

Giving a meaningful apology is one of the most important elements of taking responsibility.

A confession says, "I did it." A meaningful apology—as we teach it, inspired by authors Gary Chapman and Jennifer Thomas—involves:

1. expressing regret

2. admitting wrongdoing

3. offering restitution

4. repenting

5. asking forgiveness

The most important component of an apology? Coming forth with sincerity and humility.

———

Sharon Richardson was sentenced to 20 years to life on a murder charge. She had been trapped in an abusive relationship with her boyfriend of four months. When Sharon found out that her boyfriend molested her 7-year-old daughter, she had him killed. When Sharon went to prison, her daughter was eight years old and her son was only two.

Today, Sharon runs a successful catering business, Just Soul Catering, which makes the most delicious banana pudding I've had in my life. She also serves on the Defy faculty in a course called "The Road Less Traveled with Sharon Richardson." She shares with other EITs how she apologized to and healed wounds with her children when she was separated from them for 20 years.

Her son and her daughter regularly said things like, "I miss you, Mommy." She validated their feelings with statements like, "I am so sorry that I left you. I can see how much my mistakes are hurting you and how hard this is for you. Mommy misses you so much, too."

When there were tears, Sharon didn't run from the table. She stayed in the pain with her kids, to give them the right to process it.

"Tell me more about what you miss most about having me around." Asking a question like this, and forcing yourself to hear the child's vulnerability and heart-wrenching answers, would make cowards of most of us.

> *I wish you could pick me up at school. I wish you could read me a book at bedtime like other mommies do. I wish you could kiss me and hold me and tuck me in.*

"Mommy is so sorry for not being there for you, and for missing these important moments in your life. Mommy made some bad choices. I hate it that you are paying the price for my actions. I promise you that Mommy has made many changes so that I never have to leave you again. I promise you that when I come home, I will pick you up from school and read you books and tuck you in, and you'll get so many kisses from me that you'll never want another one again! Will you forgive me for not being there for you when you need me?"

Yes, mommy; I love you.

"For now, I know this isn't as good as my reading you a book at bedtime, but how about I write you a letter every single day, and you read it at bedtime, and know that in my heart, I'm kissing you and holding you and I'm praying for you?"

I cannot imagine the tears at Sharon's table in the prison's visitation room.

But I can imagine that because Sharon not only allowed but even encouraged and helped her kids to share their feelings, they probably didn't grow up to be a ticking time bombs. Sharon validated her children's pain and dug down into it. She said she was sorry. She said she made mistakes. She showed her repentance and could point to the ways she had used her time to change. She offered restitution. And she asked to be forgiven.

What's more, she apologized meaningfully not just once but *every time* her son and daughter's pain came up again. And her children forgave her again and again. Instead of the human pattern of lying and minimizing, Sharon established a pattern of authenticity and forgiveness, which leads to freedom.

Sharon talks about how easy it would have been to get angry and defensive and say, "I thought you already forgave me," but she understood that apologizing—and forgiving—is often not a one-and-done.

Just like when we say we've forgiven ourselves. The prosecutor in our brain will often come back to reignite the offense, and then we're left with the choice: incarcerate ourselves with shame, or reaffirm forgiveness.

"Kio, I've warned you twice. You made commitments today. Ask yourself if you're a man of your word. Please show respect to your fellow EITs. If I have to stop this exercise a third time because of you, you're out. I want you here. Ask yourself if you really want to be here."

Kio is only 19 years old. He's refusing to cooperate, turning the exercise into a joke, breaking the intimacy.

Five minutes later, I glance at Kio again. Of course, he's side-talking and laughing.

"Kio, stand up. You're out."

Ms. Hoke, you don't understand. It wasn't me ...

"Please leave. Now."

He throws his head back and has an almost proud look on his mischievous face.

Four months later, I'm back at the same prison, preparing the EITs for an event with executives. I spot Kio in a sea of a hundred EITs. How did he get into the gym? This time his head is hung; he's lost his arrogant smile.

"What are you doing here, Kio?"

Please, Ms. Hoke, give me another chance. No one has ever given me the chance that you did. I didn't understand what you were doing for me before—why you cared. No one has ever invested in me before. My dad was put on death row when I was in diapers, and I was homeless by the age of seven. Everyone I've known has abandoned me, so I couldn't understand that you would actually care about me and my future.

"What's changed? Why would I give you another chance?"

Because I've changed everything in the past four months. I stopped associating with the other youngsters in gangs.

*I don't want that. I did all my Defy homework and
assignments and watched all the courses, even though I
knew there was a good chance you wouldn't let me back in.
I'll do anything to be back in Defy.*

"Anything?"

Yes.

"Did you watch the course on How to Give a Meaningful Apology?"

Yes.

"If you're ready to apologize on the mic to all of your brothers for
being disrespectful to them, I will consider your apology."

He turned pink.

On the mic?

"Let's go."

Remember the principle that I mentioned earlier: "Keep the circle
of the confession to the circle of the sin." If I was going to consider
letting Kio back in, he needed to take ownership and humble himself
in front of those he had mocked.

He did it. Painfully, but beautifully.

Kio not only graduated Defy but is now a peer facilitator, responsible for coaching new EITs, some of whom are twice his age. He
founded a Defy Think Tank: he enlisted other youths into his group,
and they pretend they're VCs and discuss business ideas.

He's also a star performer and role model in Voices of Defy, a
spoken-word competition in which EITs express their hearts and
journeys artistically. Kio performed his poem in front of Sheryl
Sandberg, COO of Facebook, when she came to prison with us.

The story could have ended very differently, but Kio used his failure to look inside and change. He mustered the courage to come back and face me and respectfully ask for another chance. He didn't let his fear or pride stop him.

Kio said that being kicked out of Defy is what saved his life.

Kio gets out of prison in a year.

———

When we think back to the people we've hurt and the times when we haven't apologized, I imagine that we have a whole host of great excuses:

They hurt me, too.

It wasn't that big of a deal.

Time has passed; it's better not to peel the scab off.

My mistake was so bad that I can't even admit it to myself.

The person doesn't know what I did, and apologizing and admitting it would just hurt them more.

I'm scared.

I don't know how to apologize in this case.

The person won't talk to me.

The person isn't alive.

They'll never forgive me anyway.

———

This story is long, but I'm sharing the entire episode with you because it captures just how hard it can be to own our mistakes—and what it can look like when we do.

I'm angry, disappointed, and embarrassed. I want our executives to see our EITs shine. I don't love airing our dirty laundry in front of them. That's what our behind-the-scenes training days are for.

The morning had been so fun and powerful. To break the ice, the executive volunteers danced their way to the stage to introduce themselves. One of the male volunteers danced so enthusiastically that he did the splits—and right down the middle, the seam of his pants split open at the butt. What do creative entrepreneurial minds do? Use duct tape.

The day ran like clockwork. High energy and awesome.

Until lunch. We were minutes behind, so to save time, we planned to deliberate over lunch instead of taking a lunch break. During deliberation, the judges would determine which quarter-finalists would advance to semifinals. I announced that we would serve the volunteers pizza at their 15 assigned stations, where they had heard the pitches.

And that's where I went wrong.

With efficiency in mind, I asked our peer facilitators—incarcerated Defy grads who serve as role models to the new EITs—to distribute pizza to the volunteers.

While those of us who live outside the fences can probably live without a two-hour-old slice of pizza, one of our EITs told me he had not had pizza in 30 years.

At nearly all of our prisons, we're allowed to feed volunteers and EITs alike. But that day we were forbidden; we were told that EITs had to eat prison food while the volunteers ate pizza. I was steaming over the unfairness and resolved that this would never happen again (so if you come to prison with me, you will get "privileged pizza" only if the EITs do, too—otherwise, lucky you might get an authentic prison meal). But that day, I swallowed my frustration and decided I would fix this later.

So the peer facilitators, forbidden from eating pizza, were having the long-lost, oh-so-delicious pizza scent wafted in their faces and were passing the slices out to volunteers.

I absolutely should have known better.

Pizza-gate was born when several correctional officers (COs) saw five peer facilitators collude to sneak-eat an entire pie. The COs quietly called me over to inform me. Especially at maximum-security prisons, fraught with violence and riots, COs and EITs often have an us-against-them mentality.

Pizza smuggling at Defy isn't a crime. But the peer facilitators broke the directive from the prison.

Would I back up my tough talk and kick out the pizza-smuggling peer facilitators, whom I had regularly praised? Or would I look the other way? The COs wanted to see what I was made of.

I've never been a good look-away-er. I take the mic and cut the judges' deliberation short.

"I was just informed that five of you smuggled pizza. We're already running slightly behind, but until we resolve this issue and those who snuck pizza come clean, we're not moving forward. I'm dead serious."

One of the EITs raises his hand: "You're going to let pizza ruin our futures?"

"No—but you might let *lying* about pizza ruin it. Until five confess, no more pitches. No graduation."

I stand there with my mean face on. EITs stare at the ceiling with their best "It wasn't me" faces, shrugging big shoulders, throwing hands in the air, shaking heads.

The COs get frantic. My public call for self-accountability worries them, with good reason. At a maximum-security prison, when someone is accused of doing something that could put his biggest life achievement on the line, there is potential for chaos.

They thought I'd address the issue quietly. I tried that first. The COs had pointed out to me the peer facilitators they allegedly saw involved in Pizza-gate. I confronted them. They denied involvement.

I'm big on accountability, and I'm big on having a fair process.

Fifteen more COs rush into the room. Tension rises.

No one comes forward. "Fine, we'll just keep waiting."

Am I making the wrong decision by holding everyone up? Will this situation resolve? Peacefully?

I walk back across the gym to the COs and speak quietly with them.

"I'm asking you to please trust me. If I get out of line, stop me. I'm also asking you to promise that if EITs have the courage to confess, there will be zero retaliation or punishment."

The warden, Debbie Asuncion, is present now, too, and she gives me her word. Warden Asuncion is a great leader and a major supporter of Defy.

I take the mic again.

"I get it; you think I'm ridiculous. It's 'just pizza,' right? You EITs are mad at me for hijacking your glorious moment. You executives are rolling your eyes at me; I'm being petty and legalistic, right?

"But let me tell you this: I've worked harder, and for more years, than anyone in this room toward today's big event. I want this as much as you do, and this is KILLING me. I couldn't sleep last night; I was so excited for you today. We have 39 family members who have traveled all this way, and they'll be left waiting out there in the visitation room with anxiety.

"So why am I stubbornly insisting that we won't move forward until the five come clean?

"Because if I ignore it, I'll be a fraud. Executives, I twisted your arm into coming to prison by telling you that yes, my EITs have made really big mistakes, but they take ownership of their pasts. I tell the world that they are so hungry for change, so respectful, and worth betting on.

"Right now, knowing that five of you smuggled pizza hurts all of us deeply. We are all embarrassed when one of our own makes a bad decision that reflects poorly on the rest. Whoever participated, it was a bad decision—another bad decision in a string of bad decisions. And the other 55 EITs in this room who didn't smuggle pizza are mad at you for making us all look like thieves in front of these executives we want to impress.

"Is smuggling Defy pizza criminal? No. But did you break the rules that the prison set for us—whether you agree with them or not? You did. I didn't like this pizza rule either, but at Defy we talk every day about how even if we don't like the rules set by our authorities, we respect the rules.

"Do I hate the five of you who smuggled pizza? No! Will I kick you out of Defy for smuggling pizza? No. Do I have empathy for your pizza lust? Yes—if I hadn't had pizza in 30 years and had it under my nose, would I be tempted, too? Of course. You're human! And I take full responsibility for making the bad choice of asking facilitators who couldn't eat pizza to serve it. I regret my choice.

"You had a choice: respect the rules, or take something that wasn't yours."

Many EITs are hanging their heads in shame. Whether they smuggled or not, they're wearing prison blues and now are being associated with stealing—again. All the stigmas we work so hard to crush are back.

"What are you so ashamed about, Ray? Did you smuggle pizza?"

> *No. But I'm f*$!ing mad at my brothers right now. We've used up our grace. We're in prison. We want a second chance, and here they go making another mistake.*

"Raise your hand if you've made a big past mistake, and then at some point in your life, you repeated it."

Every hand goes up. Executives, too.

"Used up your grace? Really? Ray, you think you're done making bad decisions? I hate to break it to you, but you're not, and I'm not either! Defy is awesome, but it's not bullet-proof. You're going to keep screwing up for the rest of your life! Hopefully you don't screw up criminally and don't come back here, but if you think mistakes are just in your past, you're kidding yourself!

"I'm waiting for you five to come up here!"

Crickets.

Need to change up my game plan. We're 20 *more* minutes behind. What am I to do?

"The five of you—you know who you are—are drowning in shame and self-hate right now; I'm sure of it. I don't want that for you. I want your freedom. Do you want your freedom? Ask yourself that!

"Shame thrives in secrecy. When I screw up, my biggest temptation is then to lie about it, deceive, cover it up, bury my head in the sand and hope my mistake disappears. How well do those lies serve us? Even if our lies aren't discovered, we still shackle our own hearts and minds in the guilt of knowing that we not only screwed up, but then we lied. When I've done that, my mind screams at me, 'I knew you were always a failure! You'll never be loved for who you are because you're a fraud!'

"I also know the circumstances when I've had the courage to come clean. Being honest about my big mistakes has taken the most courage of my life. I fear that if I get honest, I will get the ejector seat, that I'll get lashes, and then I'll be ridiculed and publicly shamed.

"If we stand in solidarity on this, we will get to the other side, even stronger than if this hadn't happened. Let's bond in our humanity. You've heard me be a 'forgiveness parrot.' At Defy, we teach that forgiveness is a choice. It's not a feeling; it's not something we earn. We teach that forgiveness is for me; I get freedom when I choose to forgive.

"Whoever smuggled pizza, if you come clean, here is my commitment: You will not be kicked out of Defy, and I've confirmed with the COs and warden that I'll be allowed to keep you in here. I promise that you won't be ridiculed today. You also have my word that I forgive you. I forgive you for making me sad. I am just like you; I make bad decisions all the time, too, and did today. The forgiveness I would want for me: that's the same forgiveness I am extending to you."

"Executives, I'm sure some of our EITs are sweating it right now. They don't want to be labeled and written off; they feel like their futures are on the line. My million-dollar question is this: If the five guys are brave enough to come forward, do you promise to choose forgiveness; to extend them forgiveness?"

Lots of nods. The executives are all seated.

"Okay, then, executive volunteers, if you promise to choose forgiveness, please stand, and remain standing until the five come forward."

Every single executive stands. Seventy of them.

"Look, EITs, you'll be forgiven; you have our word. Who has the courage to come forward?"

At last ... one EIT comes forward.

"You ate pizza?"

Yes.

"Do you have something to say for yourself?"

I hate it that I ate pizza. I am sorry. I made a mistake.

"Joey, you are so brave to have the integrity to come clean. This is what we're all about at Defy. Second-chance entrepreneurs. I forgive you fully and completely, Joey."

He tears up. We shake hands.

Everyone claps for Joey. Everyone admires Joey. What he just did takes real courage.

"All right, volunteers, you heard Joey. If you will make good on your word to forgive him, remain standing and repeat after me, 'I forgive you fully and completely, Joey.'"

They do. It feels like we all just did church.

"Joey, thank you for modeling integrity after a mistake. Your leadership is a step in letting us move forward with our big day and celebration.

"But there are four more EITs who need to come up first. I'm pretty sure Joey and most of you know who was involved. We all know what happens to snitches in prison, so we're not asking for informants. But if you were involved, I plead with you, come up here."

Another minute of uncomfortable, exhausting silence.

Kian comes up.

"Kian, how many pieces of pizza did you eat?"

Three.

I'm super-pissed.

"Don't you do this to us, Kian. I'm giving you a chance to clean up your lie right now."

Kian is giving me the maddest look ever. He knows that I *know* he's lying.

Kian is one of our best peer facilitators. I hold him in highest regard. I'm so mad I burst into tears. "WHY, Kian? Why are you lying to me, to us, right now?"

> *I had my graduation last time around; now I want these EITs to have theirs, too, and at this rate they're going to miss it.*

Maybe Kian was trying to rescue not just the EITs and the event, but me, too. He saw the pressure I was under with the COs, and he wanted to save us all from the wrath. What Kian didn't realize is that my integrity is more important to me than anything, and I'm willing to pay any price to maintain it.

"So you just slip back to your old ways? Taking the fall for your brothers, just like you probably did to come to prison in the first place? How's that working out for you?

"You all want to know how I know Kian is lying about those three pieces of pizza?! Because during deliberation, he wasn't passing out pizzas. He was around me the whole time! I had my eye on him. Kian, WHY?"

I'm sorry.

"Yep, one bad decision, then another, then another. Are you tired of the snowball of lies? Well, guess what, Kian? I forgive you for lying. I'm hurt that you lied, but I forgive you fully and completely. Volunteers: Repeat after me if you forgive Kian."

They do.

"I'm waiting for the for-real smugglers to be men of honor."

Another minute. I'm going to faint if this keeps up.

"I think I just realized why the rest of you aren't coming up here. Even if the COs and executives and I forgive you, the other EITs might not. You're probably fearing retaliation on the yard."

Nods.

"Well, then, EITs, if you want us to be the Defy that we've all been fighting for, then it's your turn to uphold Defy's values. If the four come up here to confess, will you extend them the same grace and forgiveness that the volunteers and I are willing to give right now? Stand up if you promise to choose forgiveness and not retaliate later."

Every EIT stands.

Except Brian.

"What's stopping you?"

Mic in hand, I beeline to the one EIT who won't stand. The executives, EITs, and a whole lot of nervous COs have their eyes fixed on us.

I'm not forgiving him.

"Why not, Brian?"

I've worked harder in the past six months for my graduation, harder than anything. These thieves are ruining everything for me.

"Hmmm ... Are you comfortable sharing the crime that landed you here?"

Aggravated robbery.

"You had victims?"

Yes.

"Is it possible your robbery ruined your victims' 'everything'? Perhaps they had worked toward whatever you ruined for more than six months? Maybe there's a chance your actions even ruined the rest of their lives?"

Probably.

"Let me get this straight. You're in Defy because you don't want to be permanently known for your worst decision. You don't want that label of Aggravated Robber as your identity. These 70 CEOs and VCs here—do you want their forgiveness and acceptance? You want them having your back after release so you can get a job?"

Yes.

"You want the parole board to believe in you despite the bad decisions you've made, to give you a chance at freedom, to forgive you for your past?"

Yes.

"And let me just guess, you say you believe in a God who forgives all things?"

Yes.

"Okay."

Tears fill my eyes. I stand silently before Brian, who is clinging to his chair. I'm not mad. I'm desperately sad, desperately working toward the reconciliation between my EITs.

Other EITs start yelling. "Come on, Brian! Come on, brother, you can do it! Forgive!"

"Stop yelling at him. Forgiveness would need to be Brian's choice. We're not going to force him into it. If he chooses forgiveness, he needs to mean it."

They know I'm heartbroken. The EITs can hardly stand to see me cry.

We're now one hour into the disruption of our tightly scheduled event. All the other EITs and executives have been standing in solidarity. They chose to stand when I asked if they were ready to forgive the EITs who were "ruining" our pitch competition at California State Prison Los Angeles, a maximum-security facility where most of our EITs are "juvenile lifers": men sentenced to life in prison for mistakes they made as children. These men have grown up behind bars.

(As a side note, the U.S. is the only country in the world that routinely sentences children to life in prison.)

"Brian, I feel you. Whenever I hurt people, I want forgiveness for my mistakes. But I've been stuck in the chair like you, finding myself unwilling to forgive people when they've done things I've considered unforgiveable. If I want forgiveness for me, but I'm unwilling to extend forgiveness to others, what does that make me?"

A hypocrite.

"Brian, I forgive you. I accept you. We—this community here—forgive you and see you for who you are today, instead of for your worst decisions. Look around ..."

I turn to the anxious crowd. "If you forgive Brian like I do, keep standing, but now raise your hand so he sees and *feels* the forgiveness."

Every hand is raised.

Awkward silence; hopeful silence.

Then Brian stands. At last.

The room fills with applause—and more tears. Tears of empathy, of forgiveness, and of relief, because maybe I will finally let the pitch competition and graduation go on.

"Brian, is this you feeling peer-pressured, or is this you really choosing forgiveness?"

I forgive all of you, like you just forgave me.

I turn to the EITs. "The entire room is standing in forgiveness. I am pleading with you to be the man of courage that I know you each to be. The four of you: We're waiting to receive you and forgive you."

Two guys come forward.

Then two more.

Then five more.

Then more. And more.

Almost thirty EITs are on stage with me.

"What? I thought only five ate pizza?"

> *Yes, Cat, but a lot more of us knew what was happening.*
> *I caused a distraction on my side of the room so that other*
> *guys could eat pizza. I'm guilty.*

> *I didn't eat pizza, but I distributed it to guys who ate pizza.*

Me: "How many pizzas were eaten?"

> *Several. More than one.*

> *I let it happen, too. I should have held my brothers*
> *accountable. I knew better. I'm sorry.*

> *Me, too. I'm sorry, too.*

One by one, all 30 confess their individual participation into the mic, with offenses ranging from pizza eating to pizza distribution to being a pizza lookout or a Pizza-gate organizer or distractor.

Just like the old them.

It would be so easy for any of us to judge. "See, they will never learn." But then I think back to the Pizza-gate-style mistakes I've made in life. Repeating the past that I hate.

"Everyone repeat after me to these 30 guys—and you guys up here say it to one another:"

> *Forgiveness is a choice. I have been forgiven countless times in my own life. Though I will never stop making mistakes, I promise to do my best to learn from them so I can grow into the person I want to be. I forgive you fully and completely.*

The whole room comes together beautifully.

And then, to the 30 men on the stage, I say: "Forgiving one another is good. But it won't be that freeing if you don't choose to forgive yourself, too. Can you choose, right now, to forgive yourself for your role in Pizza-gate? Remember that forgiveness is not a feeling; it's a choice.

"Repeat after me:"

> *I forgive myself. I forgive myself fully and completely.*

They do.

"Now 30 bear hugs. You'll need them because the semifinals are on, and we have 39 family members arriving who are so eager to see their amazing, *imperfect*, forgiven CEOs of their New Lives! Let's go!"

We modify the competition a tad to make up for the 90-minute Pizza-gate. The outcome?

We ate grace.

Grace is better than pizza. Even my guys agree.

I thought some of our impatient CEOs would be annoyed with me. But nearly a year later, I got an email from a CEO who met up with another volunteer from that day. They spent their dinner reliving Pizza-gate and discussing why it was one of the most significant lessons of *their* lives.

In the six months since I'd been served divorce papers, I hadn't met up with my ex once. I was in therapy four days a week. I had gone to the leaders' screw-up camps and done a hard-core personal inventory. I was starting to take ownership of my mistakes and my past.

I didn't like what I saw.

I could have played the victim card all my life. Making my ex out as the villain, like so many divorced people do with their exes, would have been easy. Yet we each contributed to the downfall of the marriage. I wanted to do everything in my power to learn from my mistakes and to get to peace.

So I set out on a quest of writing him a letter of apology. It was so painful that it took a month to draft, edit, and rewrite. I had mentors review it to help me purge the letter of my selfishness and needs. In early drafts, I found myself justifying some of my actions, writing things like, "even though we both screwed up." In later drafts, I wiped out the self-serving excuses and defenses.

I was a wreck as I dropped the finished letter into the mailbox. I felt so naked. What if it was used against me? What about all the wrongs that he did to me? What if he never forgave me? What if he never responded?

Or worse, what if he responded with hate mail, after I had put my heart on a platter and made myself so vulnerable?

Why was I doing this, anyway?

I did it because he deserved an apology from me; he heard so few in the 11 years we were together. I did it because I wanted to take ownership of my past so I could transform my future. I did it because it was the right thing to do. I did it because I wanted to be courageous, not a scared girl in hiding. I did it because I wanted peace for myself and for him. I did it because even though the 11 years didn't have a fairy-tale ending, I wanted him to have freedom and love in his future. I wanted his future to be better than his past, even though I would not be a part of it and even though admitting this was so sad and hard for me.

When I wrote the letter, my mentors helped me resist two urges. One was to ask for a response. The other was to ask my ex to forgive me.

I felt a burning need for closure in our relationship. The end was so abrupt. I fantasized about a final "debriefing," imagining a feel-good blessing, like "let's talk about all the great memories we shared and then hug goodbye." But the need for closure was mine, not his. My mentors reminded me that if I was apologizing and taking owner-ship, I was not to ask for anything in return.

It's so easy, when we're hurting, to want our needs to be met.

What was my intention here?

I think that when we apologize, we do it partly for ourselves, but the apology won't come out right if our needs are at the forefront of the apology. When I've made an apology that is on the taking side of the equation—"I'm sorry for doing X. But you did Y, so that's why I did X in the first place"—it always blows up in my face.

Taking. Not effective.

If my primary intention with my apology to my ex was to give and to restore, then I was right in not asking for anything. Sometimes, even asking for forgiveness creates an obligation for the other party.

In general, when the apology is part of a conversation, I am a big fan of asking for forgiveness. But I had taken so much from my ex for so long that I didn't want to ask for more.

FORGIVENESS

"Step to the line if you've been convicted of murder."

One-third of the EITs are at the line. Most of them have their eyes glued to the ground; a few guys stare at the ceiling.

I feel their aloneness—even though there are 30 guys at the line.

"Pick your eyeballs up off the floor. Look across into the eyes of the volunteers. I know you hate me for calling this one out."

I turn to the volunteers.

"Why am I singling out this crime? Because these people at the line are the ones that society labels as 'monsters.' They are considered the 'irredeemable,' the 'unforgiveable.' Volunteers, you've been compassionately interacting with these men all day. You tell me: Are they monsters?"

Heads shake.

"It's so easy to write someone off and label them because of the worst moment of their lives. Most of society doesn't realize that nearly all of these guys at the line will still get out of prison. I'm proud to say that in my 12 years of doing this work, I've never had anyone who committed the crime of murder ever recidivate. Ever again. These guys have had plenty of time to look inside, to decide that they're committed to a better future.

"If I told you that I was coming over to your house with three friends—all of whom had committed murder—I'm guessing you would quickly disinvite me. Yet 80 percent of our country claims to believe in a God who forgives all things, and in scriptures that are written predominantly by three murderers: David, Paul, and Moses. How is it that most Americans model their lives by the teachings of these old-school murderers—but we permanently discard people who commit murder?

"Step to the line if you've done things so terrible that you may never forgive yourself.

"Step to the line if others have done things to you that you may never forgive them for.

"Step to the line if you are mad at God for some things that have happened in your life.

"Step to the line if you haven't forgiven God.

"Step to the line if not forgiving yourself, others, or God is hurting you to this day.

"What's stopping you? Why won't you forgive yourself?"

I pass the mic.

> *Because I am still causing pain to my family for being in here.*

> *Because what I did is unforgivable.*

"Hmmm. If you're at the line for not forgiving yourself, raise your hand if you also claim to believe in a God who forgives all things."

Nearly every hand shoots up.

"No wonder some people think Christians are hypocrites. I'm going to ask it again. Why won't you forgive yourself?"

Because I took someone's life.

I stare him down.

"You took someone's life. That was a horrible decision. I hate what you did. You hate what you did. You're in here paying the price. So, let me ask it again. Why are you refusing to forgive yourself?"

I don't know how. I've tried.

"Why hasn't it worked when you tried?"

Because I still don't feel forgiven. I guess I haven't earned forgiveness yet. I don't deserve it.

"Is there any number of good deeds, even if you lived your life as a saint for every day since the murder, that could result in your 'earning' the forgiveness?"

No.

"Not one of us will ever, ever make up for the pain we have created in the world. We all hurt people and ourselves. I hate how I've hurt so many people. I don't deserve their forgiveness. I would like to receive it. What can I do? I can't change my past. All I can do, from this day forward, is learn my lesson and live with meaning and purpose. I can live a life of love and service. That's what I'm doing here with you; it's why I started Defy. I promised God that if I ever got a second chance, I would spend my life pouring forgiveness and love into people who have screwed up like I have."

"If your victim was an emotionally healthy person, do you think they would want you tortured for the rest of your days, which only brings out evil and hatred in us and makes the world worse, or do you think they would want you living every day to make this world a better place?"

––––––––

"For those of you who stepped to the line on the question about not forgiving others—why not? Why aren't you forgiving them?"

Because the person hasn't asked for my forgiveness.

Because I'm still hurting.

Because he's still doing it.

Because he sold me out and he's the reason I'm still in prison.

"Think back to the time that you were hurt the worst by someone else. Put yourself back into that moment—when the least forgivable act was committed against you. For those of you who haven't forgiven, when you think of that person or that act, what feelings are in your heart?"

Hatred.

Vengeance.

Depression.

Resentment.

Disgust.

"How well are those feelings serving you? You want to hold on tight to that big ball of hate that's conquering your heart? You love walking around angry every day?

"Some of you think that incident was so long ago that you've forgotten it until now. Did you forget—or is the hate just jammed so deeply into your soul that you don't even realize how your hate *owns* you?

"Are you tired of not being able to sleep? Tired of the anxiety and health problems that accompany hate? Living angry? Letting your hate make your decisions for you? Think back to the last time your hate decided for you. How did that circumstance work out for you?

"When we don't choose forgiveness, we live in the ... what?"

The past!!!

"When I don't forgive, who's in control?"

The other person is! The hate is!

"So one more time, why aren't you forgiving?!"

I don't know how. I want to.

"If I choose forgiveness, is forgiveness for me or for the other person?"

For me!

Say that again if you mean it: Forgiveness is for me.

Does the other person have to ask for forgiveness for you to choose to forgive?

No.

If you forgive, does it mean that you're cool with what they did to you?

No.

If you forgive, do you have to get back into an unhealthy relationship?

No.

If you forgive, will you forget all the pain and stop being sad?

No.

If you don't forgive, who is in control?

They are.

If you forgive, do you give yourself the opportunity to transform your hustle and your future?

Yes.

If you forgive, are you giving yourself the possibility of moving forward with peace and purpose, and maybe even joy?

Yes.

Alrighty then. You know what time it is.

———

"Your elementary school didn't offer that class on how to forgive, either?"

No. Where I'm from, we learn to get even.

"Well, at Defy we teach that forgiveness is a choice. It's a decision. And it sounds like this: 'I forgive me.' Or 'I forgive him.'

"Sounds nice, doesn't it? Here's what I can promise you will happen right after you say, 'I choose to forgive': Your brain will fight you—one minute later, or maybe the next morning, but the fight is coming. The prosecutor in your brain will yell at you: 'Yeah, right! I don't forgive me! I don't forgive him! Being mad is fun! After all, he betrayed me!'

"You won't feel the warm-fuzzies of forgiveness. You'll be super tempted to revert to unforgiveness. You'll still feel the familiar burn of the hate. And your brain will keep firing away: 'Told you so! You didn't really forgive yourself! Or him either! You don't deserve it! Stay mad, you hypocrite!'

"But if you choose forgiveness over and over again, and choose to get stubborn about choosing forgiveness, and you surround yourself with a community just like this one here, a community that doesn't just preach forgiveness but practices forgiveness, then maybe one day, your feelings will follow.

"I triple-dog dare you to choose forgiveness. For you, for God, for others. And every time you think about that seemingly unforgivable act again, or every time it happens again, guess what time it is? Time to choose forgiveness again. 'I forgive me. I forgive him. I choose forgiveness.'

Can you say it with me? 'I forgive me!'"

I FORGIVE ME!

"ONE MORE TIME!"

———

My graduation speech isn't about entrepreneurship. It's about forgiveness. If there is one thing I could impart to our EITs, their loved ones, volunteers, and the corrections community, that's it. The power of forgiveness. Here's a story I've shared at recent graduations.

You tell me if this person is unforgivable. A monster. Irredeemable. You be the judge.

The 'monster' committed the crime of murder. Not just one murder. Double murder. This person killed her own mother and her mother's boyfriend. The prosecutor thought this person should get the death penalty. Plenty of Americans would cheer for the execution.

The monster has a name. Brittany. I met her at one of our women's prisons. She's serving life in prison. She hates herself to this day over her choices.

Does Brittany's backstory matter? Or were her decisions so irredeemable that no backstory could possibly matter? I'm going to tell it to you even if you don't care to know it.

Brittany was six when she started being violated by men. The violations continued until she was 13. Her mother was a drug addict. The mom's boyfriend supplied her mother with drugs. When the boyfriend raped Brittany every single day, day after day, her mom watched but did nothing so she could keep her drug supply.

Brittany was impregnated by her mom's boyfriend. At age 13.

Brittany was scared. Brittany told her mom about her pregnancy. The boyfriend found out. He beat Brittany nearly to death. The beating made her miscarry.

Brittany got more scared, scared for her life. She felt betrayed and brutalized. In her pain, she made the decision to take the lives of those who were violating her.

Today, Brittany is 25. She's been locked up for 12 years. She relives her worst decision every day. How could killing your own mother ever be forgivable? She knows what society says about her. Brittany believes society. She sees herself as a monster, too.

She is now in Defy, is in school, and has stayed out of trouble for years. But she beats herself up constantly.

If you were Brittany's guardian angel, what would you tell her? Would you, too, beat her up for the rest of her life? Or would you find it in you to tell her this? "Brittany, I forgive you fully and completely. Brittany, I don't want you shackled to the past. Brittany, you are a beautiful woman capable of living every day with dignity and purpose."

If you are able to tell Brittany that you forgive her, and that you believe she can still live a life of purpose and dignity, even from behind bars as she does her time, and that it's not too late, then can you tell yourself this?

The prison system can incarcerate only your physical self. Many people who aren't physically incarcerated choose to incarcerate themselves emotionally, psychologically, and spiritually. I believe the way to freedom is through forgiveness—of ourselves, of others, and of God.

It's so easy to be unforgiving when we don't know the human behind the label, isn't it? It's just as easy to label ourselves and to not look at our own humanity. My stuff always feels worse than your stuff. My stuff feels unforgivable.

Who would I be if I forgave myself? If I forgave him? Even when he won't forgive me?

I never did get a response to the apology letter I had sent to my ex. But I'm okay with this, right? Hadn't I convinced myself that I wouldn't get an answer? But my hurt is right here, at the surface. I had made myself so vulnerable. I'm craving forgiveness so badly, but I still don't get it. I'm tormented by remorse.

John Montgomery, who is like a father to me, says to me, "How about I stand in the gap? It won't be the same, but maybe if you hear me say the words aloud that you are forgiven, it will help you to forgive yourself. We can role-play, and I'll pretend I'm your ex."

Weird. But I'm desperate. So we set a date.

We sit outside on a beautiful day. I have a copy of the apology I had written to my ex. I read the first paragraph aloud to John.

He stops me.

> *Cat, I forgive you fully and completely.*

Weirder. I read the second paragraph.

> *Cat, I forgive you fully and completely.*

Tears are fighting their way out of my ducts.

We do four full pages just like that. I am forgiven—fully and completely—after every single paragraph.

I'm pretty hard-headed. But it's sinking in.

Sure, it's not the same as being forgiven by the person I wanted to hear it from the most. But I'm still feeling it—forgiven. Because I am. I'm forgiven by myself. By God. By John. And that's enough.

Forgiveness is my magic to start living today. It's my key to becoming the CEO of my new life.

It's graduation day. I'm armed with a different version of Step to the Line.

"Step to the line if these statements are true for you since you started Defy:"

I've taken steps toward forgiving myself.

I feel less ashamed of myself.

I've taken steps toward forgiving someone who has hurt me.

I've started the grieving and healing process.

I've become a better influence and have become more of a giver to my community and loved ones.

Today represents the biggest accomplishment of my life.

We're at the end of it. We're all whooping, hollering, in tears, celebrating transformation.

Instead of suppressing or hiding tears like they did the first time they stepped to the line, the EITs are now letting them flow. Beautiful tears of courage. Tears of freedom.

Today I forgot I was wearing this CDCR uniform. Today I forgot I was in this place. Today I feel ... human.

Forgiveness is about the forgiver as much as the forgiven. It allows us to take our attention off the past and put it on the present and the future, where it can do some good.

Forgiveness doesn't mean that the offense was okay.

When you put someone else on the hook for something that happened yesterday, you're stabbed with the same hook—reliving the pain, losing the chance for connection, and walking away from the future you could be building instead.

Forgiveness doesn't mean that there are no consequences. It merely means that you take today for what it is and for what it offers.

If a jerk cuts you off in traffic, how long does it take you to get over it, to refocus on the people you can help, not on the guy who hurt you? Your anger means nothing to him. He doesn't even know you exist. But maybe you hoard your anger all day, and you let your anger decide how you'll act when you get home to your kids that night.

Or perhaps it's the shady businessman who ripped you off for a few hundred hard-earned dollars. How does your daily mental reenactment of the crime help? You learned a lesson. He's not here. Can you forgive him enough to get your life back? After all, it's worth far more than the money he stole.

No one is suggesting the doormat model. Forgiveness is not about inviting people to hurt you again, break your heart again, disappoint you again. You're free to refuse to work with someone or to not engage with someone you can't trust.

But when we forgive someone, we open two doors: a door for them to improve and demonstrate that they have a contribution to make to others, and a door for us, to find a path forward.

RECOVERING

Now when I look in the mirror I say I love you each day.

—Michael, a Defy EIT

———

"Step to the line if you learned, by age 18, that it's better to keep your mouth shut and keep your feelings to yourself.

"Step to the line if you were taught that boys don't cry."

Nearly every EIT is at the line for both of those statements.

"There's a lot of pain, a lot of loss, in this room. When we keep our mouths shut and keep our feelings to ourselves, where do those feelings go? Do they just evaporate or disappear?"

Head-shakes.

"How do those feelings end up coming out later?"

Violence. Depression. Suicide. Drugs. Alcohol. Hatred. Self-destruction. Prison.

"So why do you think we do this exercise? It has never once been fun. I know this is hard work. If we don't learn to express ourselves with words in a healthy, safe way, is it any wonder that we use our fists? We can teach you all the entrepreneurship skills in the world, but will it do any good if you come right back here because you're a ticking time bomb, a ball of rage?

"Here's what I hear is the easiest way to do time: shut off all your emotions. Allow yourself to feel nothing. Be a rock instead of a human. How's that working out for you? Do you want your daughter to get an emotionless rock instead of a daddy who pours love out for her, the love she's been missing all these years?

"At Defy we're going to learn to express ourselves and our feelings with words so that we can thaw out and feel our humanity again."

———

Step to the line (I know, can you believe this damn exercise isn't over yet?) if these statements are true:

My parents split up, and their divorce or split deeply wounded me.

At some point in my life, I was so hopeless that I seriously contemplated suicide.

I've loved someone who died by suicide.

Violence took place in my home.

Violence took place against me.

I've lost someone I loved to gang violence.

I've lost one or both of my parents.

One of my family members was murdered.

I've seen someone get murdered right in front of me.

I was younger than 12 years old when I witnessed my first murder.

I suffered through the loss of an immediate family member before the age of 18.

I've lost a child.

I haven't properly grieved some of my losses.

The gym is so sweaty that the EITs' eyeballs are sweating. So are mine.

———

So much pain pent up inside prison walls. Two-thirds of our EITs step to the line for losing an immediate family member before the age of 18. One third for having a family member murdered. Ninety percent for violence taking place against them as children. Nearly 100 percent for having violence in their homes.

"Scott, why haven't you properly grieved some of your losses? What's stopping you?"

We don't learn how to grieve in the 'hood. We learn to get even.

Scott's jaw is clenched. He's flexing every facial and neck muscle. He's staring at me. Not in a mean way, but in a stubborn no-tears-are-ever-coming-out-of-me way and a why-are-you-making-me-go-here? way.

I've never thought about it before. If I let my wall down and started grieving, I would never stop crying. I have my entire life to grieve.

"How's that wall working out for you, Scott? Is it stopping you from feeling pain?"

Silence.

"Aren't you getting out soon, Scott? What kind of man will you be in your future if you don't allow yourself to feel? What kind of dad will you be if you can't feel love for your future kids? If you don't feel sadness when they feel sadness? You think you can train yourself to not feel for decades, and then just switch it back on in a second? What will come out of you when you finally allow yourself to thaw out?"

If we take the mask off, maybe we'll feel.

If we feel, maybe we'll grieve.

If we grieve, maybe we'll actually heal.

If we heal, we can build our new futures without being shackled by our pasts.

I received this letter from Scott midway through his Defy experience.

> *My family never showed me love or affection. Love was simply being provided the necessities of life: a roof over my head, clothing, and food on the table. No hugs, no I love you, and never a good job.*
>
> *I was taught: Boys don't cry. When I did cry, I was beaten until I stopped crying. It hardened my heart and dried up my tears. I became immune to the pain, and in some sick way, I liked the pain.*
>
> *My pain and beliefs prepared me for the streets; I wasn't scared of getting beaten up or fighting the biggest dude. I had my mask on, showing no fear, no weakness, and no emotion. I bottled up everything inside with the only outlet I knew of: violence.*
>
> *Going to prison didn't help me deal with my internal issues. It made it worse. My fear of exposure numbed me more.*

I was so numb that when the woman who raised me died, I didn't even shed a tear. My Ba Co (great aunt) was everything to me. But I didn't give myself a chance to feel the sadness or hurt. I didn't know how to grieve. Instead I drowned myself in alcohol (yes, even in prison, where we can get anything we want). I couldn't shed tears in prison—boys don't cry.

And living the lifestyle I was living just reinforced the self-limiting beliefs I was raised with. Crying in prison is a sign of weakness, and weakness gets preyed upon. As convicts, we're instructed to leave our feelings at the gate even before entering.

I've lived by this code ever since, and only since Defy have I started thinking about the possibility that my self-limiting beliefs are, in fact, limiting me. It's sad to say, but I have yet to shed a tear over the past 18 years of this incarceration, even when my uncle, grandfather, and grandmother passed away. The cold thing is, my other grandfather just passed away last month.

Grief is something I always had a difficult time dealing with, even since my transformation. All the self-help classes and talks with my support network haven't gotten me to break through to grieve yet.

I've come to the realization that I fear the grieving process. I'm scared to feel all the hurt I've suppressed all my life. I'm scared that if I start to feel again, the hurt will be so unbearable that I will not be able to come back from it. I'm scared that I will just lose complete control of myself and that I'll never stop grieving.

To this day, I'm still seeking to find the way to have the courage to grieve for my loved ones and myself. I want to be able to grieve like a normal human being, because I've stopped feeling like a human being; prison does that. I've been hoping and praying that one of these days, I'll be able to shed the tears and embrace the pain so I can heal and grow.

Defy is teaching me to work through my hurts and to use them to grow. In the course on grieving, Henry Cloud, a psychologist, said, Why do you think God put tears in our eyeballs, instead of anywhere else—like our armpits? The answer resonates with me: so others can see our hurt. We are hurt in community, and can be healed in community. I've learned from Defy that I'm not alone in my hurts; we're all hurt, and we all struggle.

Jerry Colonna, in his Defy course on The Fear of the Entrepreneur, taught me the Buddhist term dukkha (meaning suffering). He explained that we all have dukkha, and it's about how we deal with our dukkha that matters. I also am learning that my pain is not only my own; it's the next person's, too. So when I don't grieve, I don't give myself the opportunity to truly connect with another human being. With Defy, I'm starting to build the courage to be vulnerable enough to grieve and to connect with others in a powerful, life-transforming way. I'm now the CEO of my own life, and I'm prepared to Defy the odds.

We can't recover without grieving. We can pretend that we're recovering or that we're over it, but as I wrote earlier, the only way to get to the other side of the pain is to go through it.

Grieving won't make us forget. It won't stop us from feeling the pain after we grieve. But grieving does release something in us. It turns mad into sad.

Maybe you like mad more than you like sad. But how well is mad serving you?

———

So if we want to grieve, how do we do it?

I don't know that there are a ton of rules for it. But there is one: If we don't make space and time for grieving and give ourselves permission to go there, it won't happen. Period.

Skipping grieving is a promise for future disaster. Our pain-escaping minds would rather take more meetings, drink more alcohol, relapse into another bad relationship. Does escape today result in long-term escape? Or in a dogpile of pain?

I see people suffering through two kinds of pain every day:

1. Sad-happy losses

    and

2. Mad losses

Grieving a loss can look different based on the emotions we're feeling.

Say you lose your grandmother, and she was the best granny ever. I'll call this the sad-happy loss because you will be devastated to have lost her, but you generally had happy feelings about her. This loss feels fairly natural to grieve.

That's different from how Marco felt about the murder of his father.

On the life map that each of our EITs draw, Marco drew all of the major events that shaped him into who he is today. The good, the bad, and the ugly. Yet he "forgot" to include his father's murder, which happened when Marco was 16. His map had an obvious gap—the blank space during which time Marco's life seemed to go from lovely to not-so-lovely.

> *My father didn't care about me, so I didn't care about him or his murder. He walked out on me when I was a baby. I have no feelings for him, no relationship to him. His murder didn't affect me or my future, so I don't know why you think it should be on my life map.*

His words were laced with anger. Denial.

> *I don't care. Really, I don't.*

He shrugged his shoulders and seemed confused about why we cared.

Stuffing, or "forgetting," the mad losses can seem convenient. Why not try to pretend that the old hurt doesn't control us? Yet the more we fight the mad loss and tell it that it doesn't matter, the more it controls us. It chases us around, like the mad loss has a magnet to our hearts.

Why are we walking around so angry?

Think back to the last time you were betrayed, abandoned, abused, or rejected. Did you grieve it or stuff it?

So if we want to grieve, what are some ways? This isn't meant to be an exhaustive grieving manual, but here are some strategies I've learned for mad-losses:

Acknowledge to yourself first, and then to a trusted friend, that someone hurt you and that what happened is still hurting you. Instead of "I'm pissed," try "I'm hurt." Pissed rarely leads to healing.

Punch pillows or a punching bag, and let it rip until you are completely out of mad energy—not another punch left in you—and then punch one more time just to make sure you got it *all* out.

Immediately following your anger release, create a quiet space to feel the sadness. Listen to a moving song, and then do one of the next steps:

¶ Write down exactly how this person or incident hurt you and what self-limiting beliefs formed out of your pain.

¶ Decide if you're ready to choose forgiveness (even if you don't *feel* it).

¶ Write a letter (that you'll never send) to whoever created your mad-loss, and unleash your feelings of hurt. Maybe initially, you'll start by calling the person names or writing about how mad you are. But then try turning your mad into sad by writing statements like "I feel so hurt that...." If you can get from mad to sad, you're more likely to be able to choose forgiveness.

We do an exercise at Defy that you could try: First, in two minutes, in first person, tell your story aloud to a partner; describe how you were a victim and how you were hurt. Then, put yourself in your offender's shoes. In two minutes, in first person, tell his or her story to your partner, describing the circumstances that led up to this person's hurting you. That exercise *might* lead to a little empathy (but it might not).

Write a letter of forgiveness to whoever created your mad-loss. Read it every day, or read it aloud to a trusted friend, until mad turns into sad and you truly can choose forgiveness. You never need to send the letter. Forgiveness is for you. Maybe your feelings will eventually catch up with your brain, and one day you *might* actually even feel forgiveness.

And here are some strategies for grieving sad-happy losses (like beloved granny):

- Talk about the loss, especially with others who have gone through a similar experience of loss.

- Go to the person's grave. Or just have a conversation with a friend and say the words you wish you could have shared as your last words.

- Write a letter with the words you wish you had shared with the person. Read the letter aloud to a friend. Or even read it aloud by yourself.

- Go clean out the house or the person's stuff, but don't be in a hurry. Stop and read the letters or emails you received from the person.

- Look at the photos. Watch the old videos. Tell a friend about the memories, and the things you miss the most, and why you miss the person so dearly.

- Write a letter to your younger self as if you're your own guardian angel.

- Pretend you're your younger self and write a letter to the grownup you.

- Look in the mirror and pretend that the person you see is the child version of you. Let the child tell the adult what happened.

- Join a support group.

- Watch a movie about a similar loss, and allow yourself to feel and to weep. Talk about it with a friend afterwards.

- Allow someone safe to hug you or hold you as you share your pain.

❡ Make a drawing or some other artistic representation of your loss.

❡ Plan a service or celebration for the person.

❡ Pray. For yourself and for the person or their family.

❡ Write a letter of forgiveness. To yourself. Or to the person. Or to God.

———

"Why carve out so much time for my recovery? Isn't it selfish to spend all this money on my recovery?" After my scandal, I asked this of the pastor I respected so much.

Cat, believe it or not, you have a future. Like it or not, you're a leader, and you always will be. You choose what kind of voice and influence you want in the future. Do you want to lead from your pain? Or purify your influence?

Therapy, here I come.

———

A month after my scandal, I'm sitting on Dr. Henry Cloud's couch.

He's the best. And he's donating his time even though he could charge me zillions of dollars. The fact that he's giving me something that I can't pay for makes me pretty damn uncomfortable.

Think back to your childhood. When you felt pain or had a need, what did you do with it?

"I stuffed it."

Why?

"Because I learned that I couldn't depend on others to meet my needs."

How do you think that shaped who you became?

"I became the responsible one. The taker-carer of everyone else. I feel invincible. Like Rambo. Like a rock."

I want you to do something right now, Cat. Take a deep breath in, and hold it for as long as you can possibly hold it.

I do it. I start to turn a bit red as time ticks by.

Hold it for longer. Don't give up now, Rambo.

Finally, I can't hold it anymore. My breath explodes out of me. I cough and cough.

Do you see what just happened? You hold it in. For as long as you can, until you just can't anymore, and then you explode.

And here it is: the simplest explanation of what led to my scandal and to so many other self-sabotaging patterns in my life.

The next time you feel sad or alone, or feel like you might cry, I want you to pick up the phone and call a friend and tell them you feel like crying.

And here comes my second explosion—this time, one of laughter.

Cat, you just laughed in my face. Why is it that calling a friend in a time of need is so uncomfortable for you?

"I don't know. I guess because I've never been good at needing other people. Because needing people is a recipe for letdown. I'd rather just be independent."

I've always prided myself on my thick walls of "independence." How were these walls working out for me? Not too hot.

> *Hurt people hurt people. We are hurt in community, and we are healed in community.*

Who would I be if I relied on others? What other choices might I have made if I had shared my pain from the divorce and allowed people to love me in a healthy way in my time of need?

> *I have a homework assignment for you, and you're going to send me a report once a week on this. It's called your Neediness Report. At least three times every week, you're going to figure out a need that you have that someone else can meet. And then you're going to ask that person to meet your need.*

Nothing makes this Rambo girl squirm like a Neediness Report. Will I become a leech on society?

But I'm desperate for healing and recovery. I say that I'm willing to do anything to get to the other side of the pain. Am I for real about it?

I go see my mom. I curl up next to her like a cat. I ask her to caress my back. I don't remember ever asking for this as a child.

It feels ... weird. Good weird. I'm crying. Why haven't I tried this before?

Anthony, a Defy graduate, wrote me:

> *At the age of 15, I lost my father. It devastated me. I was torn. I had three brothers and two sisters and a mother, and all of them now depended on me. I couldn't understand why my father had left me to take on such a big responsibility.*

I built resentment towards him. I had so many issues, but didn't know how to deal with them.

I took my anger to the streets. One day when I was 17, I took a life. At the time, according to my gang code, I believed I was doing the right and honorable thing.

I've been incarcerated for the past 24 years. Not until just recently have I finally come to peace with myself. I now fully understand that what I did was wrong, but it took a long time to learn this because of being raised in the streets with a different moral code.

I had always shut down my emotions. Even the day my father passed away I did not shed a tear.

It's okay to feel. The day of my graduation, I was able to give my mother not only an accomplishment, but an affirmation. For the first time, I was able to shed tears. I didn't care what people said or thought of me. Defy showed me that it's okay to cry.

Also through Defy, I was able to make amends with my father, even though he had already passed. I forgave him. I spoke out loud the words I wish I could have shared with him.

Defy has taught me many things, but the most important is to believe in myself. I believed in me because Defy believed in me first. I will no longer be a disappointment to myself or others who believe in me. I am proud of who I am today. I am finally a son to my mother. A husband to my wife. A loving father, even from behind bars, to my stepson. I know I will accomplish more today than I did yesterday.

———

You are not good enough.

You will never amount to anything.

You are just like your daddy.

I knew you would fail.

You are not lovable.

You are alone and you deserve it.

If anyone knew the real you, they would spit on you.

These are self-limiting beliefs. That's shame talking.

Losing shame takes most of us out of our comfort zone because shame can sometimes feel like a comfortable, thick wool coat that keeps us in hiding.

I still hate telling my story. I've squirmed while writing it for you. I still feel naked when I tell it.

But today, I'm not incarcerated by shame. Yes, I still have guilt and remorse over my past, but that's not the worst thing. If I didn't have guilt and remorse, perhaps I wouldn't have learned from my mistakes; perhaps I would make irresponsible choices over and over again.

Sociopaths don't feel guilt or remorse. Nobody likes that. Guilt and remorse *can* be healthy for us, in certain doses, when the guilt and remorse have boundaries.

But shame? I've never seen shame be good for anyone. Shame incarcerates our minds and hearts. Shame speaks ugly messages to us—messages that we would never tolerate someone else saying to us.

———

Who would you be if you could get rid of your shame? Who would you be if the messages of shame were replaced with messages like:

You can achieve anything you set your mind to.

You are accepted.

You are safe, worthy, and lovable.

I see you, and I love you for who you are.

You decide if:

A) you want to keep your shame

or

B) you want it melting off your body to form a puddle around your feet.

If you're ready to lose the shame, that's a good first step.

Extending grace to ourselves can wash off the shame. But it's not a one-time washing process. It's a nearly-every-day process because the bonehead in us will keep making mistakes pretty much every day, and shame is always lurking, reminding us of those self-limiting beliefs, that "I told you you weren't good enough" message.

My best shame-freeing tips:

1. I don't warehouse my mistakes and hold out for one big confession like I did with the Last Five Percent. Writing that document was important to me so I could finally vomit up my dark secrets, but now when I make a mistake, I make it a priority to come clean right away.

2. Coming clean right away keeps me living in freedom. When I live in freedom, it's rare that I self-sabotage. When I respect myself, it's easier to make good decisions for myself—because I know I deserve greatness.

3. I actually practice what I preach on giving a meaningful apology, choosing to forgive myself and others and transforming my future based on the lessons I've learned.

I dare you to give yourself a shot. You deserve it.

"Step to the line if you lost your innocence before the age of 18."

About half of the volunteers are at the line; all of the EITs are at the line.

"Stay at the line if you lost your innocence before 16. Fourteen. Twelve. Age ten. Eight."

One-quarter of the EITs are at the line.

"Anyone want to share what led to your losing your innocence?"

I was found in a dumpster at age three. My mom left me there.

I flash back to pictures I have of my 3-year-old self. My curly hair was in Princess Leia balls on the sides of my head, and I had big smiles on my face. I have pictures of me chasing seagulls, camping, at the ocean, with family.

Not in a dumpster.

Had my parents—the two people who are supposed to love me most in the world—abandoned me in a dumpster, I wonder, How would I have not thrown myself away? Could I ever have learned to believe that I mattered?

"You are what you attract."

Daniella was raised to believe this. So when she attracted a man who ended up being abusive to her, she believed that she must be someone who deserved abuse. And like most EITs, Daniella was raised on the street code: Snitches get stitches. So she believed that if she ratted out her abuser and he got arrested, she would be a good-for-nothing woman without integrity. She believed she got what she deserved.

Nothing binds you except your thoughts; nothing limits you except your fear; and nothing controls you except your beliefs.

—*Marianne Williamson*

We have a Defy course called "Self-Limiting Beliefs." Teaching this course is one of the most important things we do. The process we teach involves identifying the lies that we've been told or that we tell ourselves, replacing them (in writing) with truths about ourselves (which we call "self-freeing beliefs"), and then meditating on the new truths until our stubborn brains actually believe the new stuff.

I was recently with an EIT who was being incredibly negative about himself. He was about to quit Defy because he lacked the courage to give his pitch. It was the day before graduation. He had worked so hard for six months.

"Do you happen to have your workbook on you? Will you let me take a look at your self-limiting beliefs?"

I don't have any self-limiting beliefs.

And that sums up the problem that this exercise focuses on. We usually have a serious blind spot when it comes to our own self-limiting beliefs. If we've been brainwashed with a message since the age of five, how do we even realize that we're being held back by it?

In my own life, I found it helpful to ask my friends to identify things that they thought were holding me back, things that maybe I wasn't even aware of. Sometimes our friends can hear our self-limiting beliefs coming out in our conversations when we bash ourselves or say, "I can't _____." Or, "It will always be this way."

For some EITs, the first time they got arrested as a child or were suspended from school, their moms yelled, "You're just like your father! Good for nothing! You'll end up in prison like him before you know it."

When we have an experience, it's natural to form a belief from that experience. From this belief, we form expectations. Then our behaviors often align with our expectations and reinforce the belief, and we find ourselves in a conquering cycle, creating a self-fulfilling prophecy.

I learned that we can have self-limiting beliefs about ourselves, about others ("I don't trust anyone"), and about God. We can acquire self-limiting beliefs from all types of "channels," ranging from values handed down to us from parents, friends, societal pressures, or religion to experiences that we have and things we read or see.

I started the painful inventory process of thinking back through all the negative tapes that had been playing in my head since my earliest childhood memories. I wrote down all of the messages those tapes were giving me.

A habit is more likely to sink in after repetition, so I became great at meditating on my truths—my new self-freeing beliefs—which I wrote out to replace my self-limiting beliefs. Our EITs do the same thing, and they meditate on their self-freeing beliefs for at least 30 days.

We don't just write down our new beliefs and meditate. We read them aloud to ourselves, even though it feels weird. What's even weirder is that we have EITs pair up and read their self-freeing beliefs aloud to each other.

There's so much power in having someone else wash beauty into our brains. As Dr. Cloud told me, the problem with attempting to wash the dirty water out of our own brains is that we get so used to the dirtiness that a lot of times we don't even know the water is dirty. It's just plain harder to wash our own brains.

I live in an amazing community of power washers today.

We don't get many EITs' fathers at our graduations. The room is usually filled with moms, girlfriends, wives, and kids. However, both of Scott's parents showed up at the prison for his Defy graduation.

Our graduation ceremonies include "love bombs," when EITs have the opportunity to profess their love and appreciation for their family members from the stage. Scott told me that for his traditional Asian parents, speaking words of affirmation, even in private, pretty much never happened. Speaking them *publicly?* No way. Speaking them into a microphone, in a prison?

Scott could hardly believe he was ready to break the mold.

Words of respect and appreciation started coming out of his mouth, but at last, his feelings overtook him. Tears flowed as he thanked his parents for visiting him all of these years. I wondered if his parents would be embarrassed by their son's public display of emotion, but then they willingly took the microphone and reciprocated by declaring their love for their son.

Generational patterns—broken.

I imagine what their visits could have been like all these years. And what they're like now.

I asked Scott to write down how he felt since starting the grieving and feeling process. Did he still feel like a "real man"? Did he feel whole and stable after showing vulnerability like that in a prison, in front of his peers and parents?

Scott wrote me:

> *I finally felt freed from a prison I built for myself. I felt like I could breathe again.*
>
> *After all of these years of working so hard to stay a rock, I was finally able to break free by looking deep within myself.*

It wasn't easy. There were things I didn't want to remember or feel. I was in total denial for so long, telling myself that if I didn't think about it or buried it deeply enough, it never existed.

I got tired of being numb, walking around looking like I was full of life, yet I was dead inside.

I started to allow myself to feel those past hurts and pain. I chose to trust myself to process my pain in a healthy way. It was when I embraced those feelings that I got to take off my mask. I was able to be vulnerable to the world. Doing this is what allowed me to heal from the past hurts and grow as a person.

I had never been through such an experience; I had never seen things from a different perspective. Step to the Line made me think of things I had tried to bury. I had seen the pain and hurt in others—and their courage to be vulnerable.

Seeing my peers' courage is what gave me the courage when I stood in front of my parents during my Love Bomb. I was so excited, and my emotions were very high. I had just lost my grandfather and my grandmother several months before my Defy graduation. When I opened my mouth to speak, all the pain and hurt came to the surface, and I couldn't hold it back any longer. I was hardly able to talk. Heavy tears fell from my eyes for the first time in a very, very long time.

My parents? They are proud. They are just happy they finally got their son back.

I still have my struggles daily, but today I know that if I don't deal with my emotions, it will lead to negativity. I no longer want to put on a mask. I feel that I'm strong enough to deal with anything in my path and my past. I'm proud of myself. I can now trust myself to process my grief.

Now that I've graduated Defy, I serve as a Peer Facilitator, and I mentor some of the youth at my prison who look up to me. My motto is: Learn it, live it, and give it away! I share my healing experiences with them and show them my walk. I let them know they are not alone and that we have a community that cares.

Step to the line:

"I came here today to give of myself." Every volunteer and EIT is at the line.

"What did you come here to give?"

My everything. My trust. My knowledge. My respect.

"I came here today to take for myself." Ninety percent of them stay at the line.

"What did you come here to take or to receive?"

Wisdom. Feeling alive. Meeting new friends. Connecting to others. A new chance. A first chance.

"Good! Imagine if every day, we were so intentional about living a healthy balance of giving and taking. Can it be good to take?

I tell the EITs and executives, "Imagine you save up all your money to buy a special gift for your mom or someone you love. You wait for the special day and finally present your gift, with more pride and joy than ever. But she tells you, 'Oh, son, I can't take this from you. Please return it.' How do you feel?"

Sometimes when people can't take, it hurts.

And have you ever known someone who gave with unhealthy motivations, and what they were doing was actually taking? If I give in order to receive something in return, am I really giving?

Think about it. In recovery, we need a healthy balance.

I know that when I give from a healthy place, even when I expect nothing in return, I feel alive and fulfilled. I know that when I am just purely taking, day after day, I feel like a leech. And I disrespect myself. So part of my recovery was finding small, meaningful ways to give.

"What's the most recent small way an EIT in this gym gave to you, maybe even today?"

He smiled at me.

He gave me a good bear hug.

He called me by my name.

We have no excuses not to give. Our opportunities are everywhere!

When we're in recovery, our normal stance is usually to be in taking mode. We've probably just done a whole lot of taking with our mistakes, and then it's natural to become needy and self-absorbed when we're recovering and healing.

Some people think all taking is bad. Is it?

Was it bad that for a year after my scandal, I focused on recovery and spent so much effort on my own therapy four days a week? In my therapist's office, I can assure you that I was 100 percent taking. I sucked every session dry.

After devoting my life to PEP, I knew that to become whole again, I needed to start taking. In fact, my Weekly Neediness Report was an assignment in taking.

Most EITs come to Defy taking. I don't expect anything different.

And then there's that moment when giving becomes just a natural part of us. What we've been craving to do all along.

"Do you understand that you chose that seat?"

Carter, a Nebraska EIT, was furious. He was in the seat reserved for the guy who does the most taking.

We were seated in a circle, doing Giving and Taking, a not-so-fun awareness-building exercise, at an Omaha prison.

We start with talking about the feelings we experience when someone is giving to us.

Happy. Grateful. Treasured. Known. Valued.Connected.

Then the feelings we experience when someone is taking from us without our consent.

Betrayed. Used. Angry. Vengeful. Skeptical. Violent.

An EIT scribe is writing all of these feelings on the board.

The EITs get stacks of voting tickets. The orange tickets represent Taking. The green tickets represent Giving.

"You're going to go around the circle, plant your feet in front of every man here, look him in the eye, and say only the two following things: his name, and either the word 'giving' or the word 'taking.' Don't overthink this. In the moment, when you stand in front of the man, if you experience him as giving, hand him the green ticket and say, 'Name, giving.' If you experience him as taking, hand over the orange ticket and say, 'Name, taking.'

"You all did a great job of shouting out the feelings you experience when someone is giving or taking, and you all know each other after living with each other. Think of how each man makes you feel. If you stand before the man and you know that interacting with him brings you happiness and gratitude, and makes you feel valued and connected, give him a green ticket. If you stand before him and find yourself unsure, then it's orange. If you don't experience the positive feelings, then say, 'Name, taking.'"

The tough guys squirm. "What? I don't understand." All types of objections. Their brains start to act "confused." Confusion can be a cover-up for resistance.

"Yes, I'm going to force you to stop in front of each man, look him in the eye, and make a choice. Stop your squirming. To me, this feedback is a form of respect. Do you realize we make these choices every single day? But often, we make these choices behind people's backs. We cut people down in conversation. Or when someone is walking toward us, we pretend we don't see them and walk the other way. We dismiss people all day long. Would you rather be stabbed in the front or the back?"

The front.

"That's what I thought. But this isn't a stabbing. This is honest feedback. This is us living out one of Defy's values, Love Hard. Now start."

Once they've all gone around the circle, they also give themselves a ticket and loudly proclaim their own name and either "giving" or "taking" in front of the room. Then they count up the tickets they received—how many orange, how many green. The men all stand, and we rearrange their order as follows:

"Anyone have 40 orange tickets? You sit on this end of the circle. Thirty-nine orange? Here, next to him." And so forth, so the guys with the most Taking tickets are all on one side of the circle, and the guy with the least Taking tickets (and the most Giving tickets) is the last one to sit down.

———

Carter wouldn't stop his protest.

I didn't pick this seat. This was rigged.

"Carter, can you think of anything you might have done, or omitted to do, or maybe body language or words you've used, that could have led any of your brothers to give you a Taking ticket?"

Nope.

"Do you have a parole date?"

Nope. I saw the parole board last month and they turned me down. Again.

"If there were any parallels between this exercise and the way your brothers perceive you and the way the parole board perceives you, and you could gain awareness of the energy you're giving off and then have a chance to fix it, would you want to know?"

I guess.

"Guys, this isn't a snitching thing. Carter isn't getting into trouble here. If you love him, you will have the courage to tell him why you gave him a Taking ticket. Thirty-six of the 40 of you gave him Taking tickets. Out of respect for him, tell him what he did, said, or didn't do or say that led you to give him that ticket."

Ten EITs shoot their hands up and give Carter straight feedback.

"How does hearing all this make you feel, Carter?"

Why did it take so long for all of you to tell me this stuff? Maybe I would have made parole if I had known all along I was coming off as such an asshole.

"How many of you just heard this acknowledgement—this awareness—and experienced Carter' admission as a Giving action?"

Almost every hand shoots up.

"Carter, usually the EIT in the most Taking seat remains in pure denial. They're so used to taking, taking, taking and then get so defensive and angry for being 'revealed' that they just take more. I find your ownership of your taking actions to be refreshing.

"Carter, you took our courses on forgiveness and giving meaningful apologies, right?"

I was about to suggest that he carve out time to apologize later for whatever taking actions he could remember, but he beat me to it. He stood up and started running around the circle, tapping most of the guys on the knee, Duck-Duck-Goose style.

"What did you just do, Carter?"

> *If I just tapped you on the knee, it means I know when I took from you. And later, in private, I want to have a conversation with you to apologize. And for the rest of you that I didn't tap, if you gave me a Taking ticket, I would like to know how I took from you, so I can apologize to you, too.*

This was a first.

Carter made parole a year later.

———

Part of our recovery process is gaining painful awareness. Why did we make our choices? What led to them? Why do we keep getting passed up for opportunities? Why is the parole board—or our daughter—or our boss—rejecting us?

One of my friends says, "The brain can't be curious and angry at the same time."

It takes a mountain of courage to invite honest feedback like Carter did. And when we receive it, to just take it in—instead of getting defensive, then recovery can truly begin.

———

Jason was in the #1 Giving seat in the circle.

"Jason, do you know that you chose that seat, just like Carter chose his?"

Jason looked horribly embarrassed, like he had done something wrong. He started crying.

"Why are you crying? Every one of your brothers gave you a Giving ticket. Do you see the board over there with all the positive feelings you seem to consistently create in your brothers? Why are you embarrassed?"

I don't deserve this.

"Don't deserve what? To be recognized for the giving you're doing?"

I killed someone.

"And you're in prison because of it. You are paying your debt to society. Because of a big past mistake, do you need to be cruel to yourself for the rest of your life?"

He could hardly speak.

The EITs went around sharing examples of Jason's giving nature.

MOVING FORWARD: REINVENTING YOURSELF

Most people don't change a thing, because change—transformation, reinvention—takes deep courage, humility, commitment, effort, and time.

It takes admitting that we didn't have it figured out the last time around.

It involves finding the time to recover and embracing the process.

It involves asking for help.

It involves being vulnerable.

It involves a decent possibility of failing all over again.

———

What does it mean to reinvent yourself?

The U.S. calls itself a free country. Yet I know plenty of free people who act as if they've been sentenced to Life Without Parole.

When I speak at companies, I ask, "How many of you are living your dream, your dream job; you feel fulfilled?" Maybe 10 percent of the people in the audience raise their hands. And yes, it's pretty awkward because their bosses are in the room.

Why only 10 percent?

Perhaps they hate their jobs but feel trapped by their salaries or by having just a few more years until retirement. Or maybe they hate their spouses and say divorce is not an option and claim that "it's better for the kids" if they stay in a hateful or apathetic marriage. Or maybe they hate their cities and hate being single but won't consider moving because home is safe and easy and just the way it's always been.

Do you ever think about why so few of us do what we want? Do you stop to think about what's in the way of getting what you want?

I know plenty of Defy Lifers in prison who live with more mental freedom than some people on this side of the fence do.

If you aren't living with fulfillment and haven't yet figured out your Generous Hustle, as I call it, read on. This book isn't a quick fix or just words of inspiration. It also isn't a promise of results, unless you commit to the discipline and hard work required to figure out your Generous Hustle. Getting there is worth it. Through Defy, I've guided thousands of people with criminal histories through restarting their lives, even after catastrophic failures. They get to the other side and find fulfillment and meaning—their Generous Hustle. If they can do it, maybe you can, too.

What's been stopping you? Some answers I get:

I don't even know what my ideal job or life looks like.

I don't know where to start.

I would have to start all over from scratch.

I don't really feel like I have a choice.

I'm a slave to my bills.

I'm scared to try something new.

I don't have the right connections.

I don't have the ____ that I would need to do what I want to do.

I'm in a rut and don't have the energy.

I'm locked up (physically in prison, or financially, mentally, or emotionally imprisoned).

This is for you if you're willing to lose the excuses.

This is for you if you're willing to get uncomfortable.

This is for you if you're willing to make and keep a commitment to get to the other side.

This is for you if you're willing to stop being a spectator.

The enormity of your setbacks and obstacles doesn't define your future. Your attitude about them does.

———

At Defy, we spend a lot of energy on discovering our gifts, passions, and Generous Hustle. We have a course called "Develop Your Dream." Another called "Living a Life Well Lived." We take personality assessments to identify our strengths and weaknesses.

One of my favorite ways we start to figure out our Generous Hustles is to begin with the end game: writing our eulogies.

EITs start with Eulogy #1: the reality of today. If you died today, what would be the honest, hard truth about your life and impact? They write it in two pages or less, from the perspective of someone who would read it at their funeral.

Then it's time for Eulogy #2: the life well lived. We provide them with guidance and questions that help them to create their ideal, but realistic, life plan and impact.

The third part of the exercise is the most important.

They write out the ten most important changes they need to start making in their lives today to get from Eulogy #1 to Eulogy #2. Then they prioritize the changes and commit to three changes they will make, starting today.

Then they learn about SMART (specific, measurable, achievable, results-focused, and time-bound) goals. Then they put their SMART goals in writing, sign their names to them, and get accountability partners.

That exercise gets us moving in the right direction.

I triple-dog dare you to do it, too.

―――――

"Step to the line if you're a natural-born hustler."

Nearly all of our EITs are at the line.

Whether or not you consider yourself to be a natural-born hustler, if you've made it this deep in the book, you've got some hustle—own it!

When I talk about finding your Generous Hustle, I mean discovering the thing that makes you feel alive, the thing that makes staying alive feel worthwhile, and doing that thing for someone else.

If we only hustle for ourselves, our hustling can become selfish. But when we choose to hustle for someone else, for the community, for those we care about, the outcome can be powerful, purposeful, and life-giving.

After we've screwed up, it can be easy to feel like a loser, like we have nothing to live for. But you know that this isn't true. You have something left to give, even when you feel the emptiest.

When I write about a Generous Hustle, I typically refer to it as your vocation—what you do for a living—but it can easily be a side hustle, too. Most people can't afford to immediately quit their day jobs to pursue their dreams. But if your day job is allowing you to participate in a fulfilling side hustle, then it can make getting through the day entirely worthwhile.

When I talk about your Generous Hustle, I'm talking about that thing that:

- Makes you excited to get out of bed on a Monday morning

- You dream about at night

- You have a hard time shutting off when you're on vacation

- You would do even if you won the lottery

A Generous Hustle could be:

- Running your own business or nonprofit—that company you've always wanted to start, but haven't had the guts to do it, and now you start it during your weekend or evening hours

- Volunteering with a nonprofit or faith-based organization in a capacity that is meaningful to you

- Leaving your nice salary to do something that pays dirt but makes the world a better place—and makes you happier than your paycheck did

- Mentoring the people who work for you, for their sakes

❡ Engaging deeply in parenting—and stopping doing something else that is taking you away from being the parent that you want to be

In a bit, I'm going to dare you to do things that you've been too chicken to do—the very things that might be keeping you from fulfillment, that might keep you underutilized or even bored.

And now, a special note to all my currently incarcerated brothers and sisters:

You might be at the low point of your life. Prison is where people can learn to live without hope. I'm hoping to stir that hope back up, and it's not fluff. It's the solid hope you can build a future on.

What do you have to lose? When we don't have a lot to lose, we are willing to be brave, and we are hungry for a new way—anything other than what we're doing today. This is why bringing hope to prison is my favorite journey in the world.

How I wish people in the free world shared your mentality and your hunger for a new life!

Think of it this way: Pretend you have a $500,000/year job, but you absolutely hate it and you work 80 hours a week. It keeps you on the road, away from your family. But your wife and kids grow accustomed to your income—private schools, a big house with big bills. You have a lot to lose. You can't just walk away from your job—you feel trapped. And with 80 hours a week of work, you don't have the time—or the energy—to dream about anything else. Lifestyles, and salaries, can be so addictive.

Or say you're that kid with the 4.0 GPA. You've always brought home straight A's, and that's what mom and dad simply expect of you. You're terrified of getting a single B. You would like to try out a new creative class, but you're not sure you would ace it. So you never try anything new or courageous. You're trapped in a psychological prison.

If you're willing to fail, you also have a chance at winning. Finding and developing your Generous Hustle requires getting outside of your comfort zone and taking risks. Scary stuff.

When you're incarcerated, you have the time and space to reinvent yourself. As horrible as your conditions may be in prison, you can choose to make the most of your timeout by investing your energy in a better future.

We always have more than enough legitimate reasons to complain and to be unhappy. Or as I say to our tough guys at Defy events: "Did you get some feedback that you didn't like? Didn't win the pitch competition like you thought you would? You now have a choice. You can suck your thumb all the way back to your bunk and decide that Defy is rigged, and drop out. Or you can suck it up, incorporate the feedback, and come back stronger the next time."

Sometimes I hear from incarcerated people that they feel like they don't have choices in prison. But we all do. The system can only incarcerate your physical self. Only we can incarcerate our hearts and minds. Defy's program in prison is called CEO of Your New Life ... because you are.

If you're incarcerated, use this time to transform your hustle and to identify your Generous Hustle—to discover the person you were created to be. I know you can do it. And the reason I would rather be in prison than anywhere else on any given day is that every day in prison, I am surrounded by courageous, willing souls who do whatever it takes.

This is why Defy just rolled out a new program for Lifers; it's called The Marathon. All the entrepreneurship skills you'll learn in CEO of

Your New Life? You can still use them. You can't start a legal business from inside prison, but you can start a program, a nonprofit that makes your world a better place. We have incarcerated grads who are amazing artists who have started art classes for other incarcerated people through The Marathon. We have a young grad named Jesse who started a mentoring program that closes the age gap; incarcerated 25 to 30-year-olds mentor incarcerated 18 to 25-year-olds. We have grads who have started parenting classes. And on and on.

When Marathon EITs come up with a curriculum and a methodology that together produce a proven social impact in their prison, they can pitch their idea in our Marathon competitions. Winning ideas are nurtured and given a chance to grow. Defy can take those programs and spread them to other yards, other prisons, even other states.

Even if you're locked up for life, you can still live a life of love and service. You can find and develop your Generous Hustle. Just lose the excuses and start asking what you can do today to make a positive difference in one neighbor's life.

Someone once told me the definition of hell: On your last day on earth, the person you became will meet the person you could have become.

—Anonymous

———

"Only five of you will survive. The rest of you? Welcome to the last two hours of your life. You have 45 seconds to stand up, state your name, and explain why you want a seat on the lifeboat. Then you sit down and the next man makes his case. If you want a shot at being chosen for a seat on the lifeboat, make your very best case. Why should this group pick you to survive, out of the 50 of you?

"First man, stand. Your 45 seconds start now."

The EITs pretend they are on a dream voyage they had awaited all their lives: a ship that is supposed to take them around the world. But the voyage fantasy turns dark. Titanic-style, they're now imagining the icy waters that will take their last breaths.

I'm Rudy, and I want a seat on the lifeboat. I've been in prison for 20 years, but I have five kids out there who need me. I hope I go to the parole board next year. I need to be out there, man.

I'm Joe, and I don't deserve to live. All I've done with my life is make mistakes and let people down. I won't be going on the lifeboat.

I'm Cody, and I'm giving up my seat on the lifeboat. All I've done with my life is go to prison, and I don't have kids, so I want to give my seat to someone with kids who can go out there and make a difference.

Maybe one-third of the guys say they'll give up their seats on the life-boat. Some of the seat-forfeiters have a heroic tinge in their voices as they proclaim that they'll sacrifice their seat for someone else.

Everyone has given their pitch.

"Cody, I heard you say you are giving up 'your' seat. But in the instructions, did I tell you that you had a seat in the first place? What made you think you had the power to give a seat to someone else, or that any seat was yours to begin with?"

Cody crosses his big arms and squints at me.

"Imagine if my instructions were: You *have* a seat on the lifeboat. You're on your way to safety. Now decide if you want to remain as one of the five survivors, or pitch yourself overboard into the freezing water to give your seat to one of the 45 who have already started drowning.

He's breathing heavy.

"Instead of making a case for your life and future, you committed suicide."

What? No I didn't.

"You quit on yourself. And you attempted to cover it up with a heroic twist, acting like you were giving up a seat that you never had.

"How might this exercise have some parallels with your real life?"

The exercise opens up new ways to see ... to see others and to see ourselves. Do we have a seat on the lifeboat? What are we doing with it?

Now imagine you're safely in the lifeboat, one of the five survivors, on your way to land.

If you were one of the five survivors, how would you live the rest of your life? Would you act differently to honor the people who didn't get a seat, especially if one of them tossed themselves overboard just for you, because they believed in your future and they were willing to die so you could truly live?

———

What about your life today makes it worth living, worth betting on?

When I'm doing something awesome, it's easy for me to make a case for the lifeboat. But right after I screw up? Not so clear that I want or deserve a seat.

After I screw up, I have a choice. I can pity myself. Or I can tell myself "I screwed up and I own it, but I'm the CEO of my new life. I lost some opportunities and am suffering consequences, yes. So I'm reinventing a part of myself. I'm learning from this experience to become a better person."

If you knew right now, with confidence, that you were holding the keys to others' futures, would you pitch yourself into the icy water, keys and all? Or would you commit to reinventing yourself, so you could bring beauty into the lives of others and start living a life worth living?

———

Reinvention sounds scary.

You don't need to figure out your whole life purpose right now. But having *a* purpose—a reason, any reason—to even get out of bed in the morning—let's start there.

It only takes an ounce of purpose to begin. Just a few drops to start moving.

Once we've been defeated, embarrassed, shamed, we easily lose our bounce-back. After my resignation, mustering the courage and energy to start another organization seemed impossible. I was just exhausted and defeated. I needed that year of therapy and time off to reinvent one small part of myself at a time.

Reconnecting with an ounce of purpose can give us energy when having energy seems impossible. For instance, if I know that I can be a friend to you by listening to your pain, that's purpose. If I know that I could write a letter to my friend today and that she might be encouraged by my words, that's purpose. If I know that my brothers could use me on the basketball court because they are more likely to win if I play, and winning makes them feel good, that's purpose, too.

What could you do today that could give you even half an ounce of purpose?

Build up your purpose.

Create some purpose today. Then tomorrow. Then every day this week.

See how you feel as you live generously. Keep a daily purpose log, and make sure you make a contribution to someone each day.

At Pelican Bay last week, I launched a Kindness Competition. Our EITs—even those in solitary confinement—now have a Kindness Log, and they're keeping track of random acts of kindness for their peers, and even for uniformed staff. When they get a food tray in their feeding slot, instead of saying nothing, now they are thanking and acknowledging the COs for their service. In two months, the

EITs will give a presentation about their boldest acts of kindness, and how it impacted them and those around them.

How might your day change if you were intentional about kindness and generous acts?

Generous living isn't just about money. Sure, you can be generous financially. But you can also be generous with your smile, your time, your listening ears, your hugs, your written and spoken words, and your talents.

I'm pretty sure every human is hard-wired with a deep need to love and serve. When we love and serve from a healthy place, that leads to fulfillment for us.

Once you build the habit of living with an ounce of purpose every day, start noting the impact it has on you. When you smile at others, do they smile back, at least sometimes? Does it make you happy to make others happy?

Once generous hustling becomes part of your daily routine, you'll be ready to move on to bigger steps.

———

If you felt passionate about a beautiful, transformative, important Generous Hustle, it could change everything.

You would fight for your Generous Hustle just like a mother would fight to protect her newborn. You wouldn't be fighting for your own need to live—you would fight because you would know that your impact on others is significant and needed.

What kind of Generous Hustle would you need to live to make sure that you wanted a seat on the lifeboat?

Pick me because I've never really lived before.

Okay, but how much more compelling would that pitch be if it was:

> *Pick me because I haven't really lived before, but if you give me a chance, I'm 100 percent committed to doing x, y, and z, and my impact will be a, b, and c?*

Committing to your Generous Hustle will make you feel worthy, more powerful, more generous, able to become the person you hope to see in the mirror. You will feel it in your bones.

Your Generous Hustle could be all about creating beauty in your children's lives. We can't make up for the past, but even if your kids hate your guts today, it doesn't mean that you can't win them over in time. But if you don't even try, you'll never know!

My life is about helping other people become more powerful and creating opportunities for them to live a life that is truly their Generous Hustle, their fulfillment of who they were created to be.

In the times that I've done this lifeboat exercise, the people who consistently get picked for the coveted lifeboat seats are the givers. These givers contribute to the lives of others every day. They also give to themselves and know that their lives are significant.

The takers fight so hard for the seats—so selfishly—but no one wants the takers in the seats.

Who do you know who would be worthy of a seat on the lifeboat? What are the things that person does that makes them worthy of that seat?

If you make a list of all those people and all those things, maybe some patterns will emerge. The things you value and respect, these are perhaps the qualities, the choices, you want for yourself.

You may have no idea of what your Generous Hustle will be. You're not alone. Plenty of people don't.

The things that would make you most pick-able for that lifeboat are probably the same things that will provide you with the greatest sense of fulfillment and joy.

Ready to explore what that could look like for you?

———

If you died today, why would your life matter?

The rich CEO in front of me can't believe I'm asking him that question. He's fumbling nervously. He's not satisfied with his answer or his life.

Whenever I've asked this question before, the best answers all shared one theme: Mattering doesn't come from what they've done or achieved for themselves. It doesn't come from the dollars accumulated or the companies built or sold. Mattering always comes from what they do for others. Service.

Hiring someone who wasn't given a chance anywhere else.

Sacrificing for their daughter so she can attend the college of her dreams.

Moving across the country for his wife so she can pursue her promotion.

It's why so many executives get addicted to Defy. They matter every minute when they are sharing and contributing love and care and hope into my guys.

———

A man on the sidewalk is frightening me. He's violently throwing his hands around, cursing like a madman.

He has just discovered that his new Porsche got keyed.

I flash back to last year when my derelict junker didn't just get keyed; it got a basketball-sized dent. I thought, "Oh well. Maybe I'll get that fixed someday."

Does this crazy man own his Porsche? Or does the piece of metal own him?

––––––

If we try to figure out our one big life purpose, we'll be paralyzed. We need to start small. Tiny, even.

I started by just writing down one or two ways my life mattered that day: I smiled at a stranger to make him feel noticed. I opened the door for a disabled person.

When I was at my bottom and couldn't see above the clouds, I had no idea how I would stop being embarrassed for being alive. When I was a participant instead of the leader in the lifeboat exercise shortly after starting Defy, I found myself saying:

> *I'm Cat. I previously wouldn't have wanted to be on the lifeboat, because I hated myself so bad that I didn't want life. But now that I'm experiencing my second chance, I promise that if you all choose to entrust me with a seat on the lifeboat, I will bring my everything into creating second chances, and third chances and three-hundredth chances. I don't have kids, but I will do all I can to create training for moms and dads that will make sure they reconnect with their kids, so these kids can have new legacies. I will do everything I can to make sure Defy is in every part of the*

*country, defying statistics of failure and creating stories of
beauty and redemption nationally.*

This book is my best attempt to make good on that promise.

———

*Cat, every single day that you spend not doing what you feel
like you're designed to do is a wasted day in your life.*

That was the push I needed. I hate waste.

I was telling Marc, my venture capital colleague, my vision for launching PEP, saying that this work was the passion of my heart. That I was so excited I couldn't sleep at night. I was spending fifteen hours every weekend editing EITs' résumés for fun.

But I was scared, so scared. Who quits a good finance job at 26? I had no idea how I would financially support myself if I pursued my dream. I had no experience starting or running an organization. Some of my advisors told me I was wasting my potential with this "prison stuff." I had a million excuses.

For most humans, self-preservation is a greater need than fulfillment, adventure, or even doing the right thing. Had I relied only on these "responsible types" for advice, I would have stayed an unfulfilled coward.

It was time to start getting advice from people who I actually want to be like when I grow up.

The people I spend the most time with now are other calculated-risk takers. Other world-changers. People whose dreams are bolder than mine. They don't just tell me to take the plunge; they do it themselves on a regular basis.

This part of the Franciscan prayer kept eating at me: "May God bless you with enough foolishness to believe that you can make a difference in this world, and in your neighborhood, so that you will courageously try what you think you can't do."

The next day I walked into the managing director's office at my investment firm and told him I was leaving New York City to start PEP in Texas.

What would it take for you to walk away from your comforts?

Change happens when the pain of staying the same is greater than the pain of change.

—*Tony Robbins*

One of the main ideas behind Alcoholics Anonymous is that you have to hit bottom first—before you can change. If you haven't bottomed out like most of my EITs have, it might take a lot more discipline for you to take the plunge. You'll likely have more to lose and farther to fall.

What do you need to lose in order to get to fulfillment?

What are the payoffs that make you stay in your prison?

Why is it so hard to convince unfulfilled people to walk away from unfulfilling careers when there could be so much more?

Because our brains feed us excuses—with a hint of truth in them. If the excuses were invalid and didn't contain truths, they would be easy to dismiss.

You decide what is more important:

A) Your need for safety and self-preservation

or

B) Your need for fulfillment

These may not always be mutually exclusive. But if you have to prioritize, which is it: A or B?

Defy serves some people who have been sentenced to life without parole. They can't start a legal business inside. Does that stop them from living their Generous Hustle? No.

I've heard plenty of people say, "It's like I'm in prison." I don't know your circumstances, but I'm guessing it's *not* like you're in prison, even though you may live that way and tell yourself that.

It can be easy to feel like our power is stripped by:

- Significant others
- Parents
- Addictions
- Finances
- Religions
- Cultural expectations
- Setbacks
- Location
- Physical health

We tell ourselves that we can't do X because of Y.

But it's often not that we can't do X; it's usually that we choose not to see a way around Y, persuading ourselves that a way might not even exist. Or sometimes don't know a way around Y even exists, or we don't know how to get there. We all have some limitations, whether physically, financially, or otherwise. Can we have everything we want? No. But can we still develop a Generous Hustle, regardless of our limitations? Absolutely.

People who aren't behind bars can typically change most circumstances (there are exceptions, of course). When they don't, it's typically because they don't want to change it.

Is it a prison if we choose to stay in it and we hold the keys to our own cell?

Let's do some unlocking of common excuses:

Wanting more money

I'll wait until I'm rich or older.

I just want to make as much money as I can until I'm 40. Then I'll settle down and start giving back. Right now, it's just about me. That's like saying that I'll eat my way up to 400 pounds, and then next year, I'll cut back to 150 pounds.

Greed feeds more greed. Does anyone ever feel rich enough?

I don't have the money I need for my Generous Hustle.

If I had expected Defy to be a national organization on day one, I wouldn't have had the money to do it, either. What do you have enough money to do now?

When I was starting PEP, I knew I would need more money than I had. My former husband and I lived in a one-bedroom apartment in New York City. To cut expenses and save up for my Generous Hustle, we slept on an air mattress in the kitchen three nights a week while renting the bedroom to a commuter.

What can you live without in your current budget, so you can start saving money now?

> *I'll wait until I have enough savings in the bank and am set up for retirement.*

That day will likely never come.

If you don't commit to your Generous Hustle, why would anyone else commit to it?

Living your new Generous Hustle will almost always involve a financial investment and risk. If you have to switch careers to do something more fulfilling, you might have to start at the bottom. If you coach a team on the side, you might have to forfeit overtime pay at your full-time job.

Fearing failure

Is the truth that you truly can't afford it, or is your fear of failure controlling your future?

> *I've never done anything else and am terrified of failing.*

> *I don't want to disappoint my parents, and keeping my parents proud is more important than being fulfilled.*

What's the real tape playing in your head?

I wrote down the tape of self-limiting beliefs that was playing in my head, and they were far uglier on paper. Then I even confessed my beliefs to someone. And once I was out of the closet, well, I had to take action.

My amazing mentor, Seth Godin, wrote a blog post called, "How do I get rid of the fear?"

> *Alas, this is the wrong question.*
>
> *The only way to get rid of the fear is to stop doing things that might not work, to stop putting yourself out there, to stop doing work that matters.*
>
> *No, the right question is, How do I dance with the fear?*
>
> *Fear is not the enemy. Paralysis is the enemy.*

I have a serious fear of failure. But greater than that is my fear of not living my Generous Hustle to the fullest. I just committed a long time ago to not letting my fear stop me. It's really that simple.

Fear is human and normal and even good. Failure is no fun, but failure isn't the end. Some failure is generally required if we really want to get to something great.

If you're waiting to get to a point where you aren't scared anymore, you'll never arrive.

Feeling alone

You're so sad that you feel like you can't take a step, but part of the solution is to take a step. Maybe this will help: No one said you had to take the step by yourself. This is where getting an accountability partner—a motivator—might get you there.

"Thank you for making me feel human for the first time in a long time." We hear this from EITs all the time.

When we feel our humanity, and feel like we're doing something that matters, we start to realize that we do matter. Sometimes we have to be seen by others for the first time—perhaps differently from the way we've previously been told we've been seen—so we can finally see ourselves. Find someone who sees you and will motivate you to take baby steps.

Not having the right experience

Don't you think I need a few years of real work experience first?

Good experience rarely hurts. The only problem with needing more experience is that it's really similar to the excuse of needing more money. When you take a risk to start a new hustle, you'll never have enough money or enough experience.

Most people I know who get an MBA get it because they're scared of feeling inadequate without the degree. They're buying two years of time, at an extremely high price, so they can figure out their hustle.

I'm not anti-education and I really like to hire people with MBAs. But if there's a more efficient way to get from A to B, why not just take that route?

Say that becoming a doctor is your vision for your Generous Hustle. Why do you want to be a doctor? To save lives?

It will cost you seven (or more) years of your life and more than $300,000 in tuition debt plus interest (not to mention the foregone income for those years). If your Generous Hustle can be fulfilled only by you personally doing every single surgery, then I guess you better start saving up and studying for the MCAT. But what if a faster way for you to get from A to B is to start a company that gets doctors to donate time pro bono to low-income patients?

Is there a more efficient way to achieve your Generous Hustle?

Some of my most dissatisfied friends are lawyers. They "can't afford to leave their jobs." If your Generous Hustle is about defending the law or fighting for the rights of others, and you don't yet have a law degree, can you find other ways to reach those goals?

If you already have a degree or have professional experience, then you have fewer excuses. Your experience can be a great asset to your future, even if it's not directly relevant.

Think about my EITs. Nearly all of them have experience as drug dealers. They transform their hustles from illegal enterprises into legal ones. But the EITs are still able to start awesome legal companies—without MBAs.

Fearing success

Almost as paralyzing as the fear of failure is the fear of success. It's the reason that we make our Generous Hustle plans so big. The reason we create impossible goals. The reason we sabotage our work so regularly.

Because if we succeed, we've changed. And change is scary.

Because if we succeed, we're unprepared. A fraud. Unentitled to what's happening.

It's easier to fail.

Worrying about other people's opinions

Everyone, particularly my immigrant father, thought I had lost my mind when I left a New York City private equity job for prison.

The biggest deal-killer isn't what other people say about us, though; it's what we tell ourselves about what they say to us.

It's not that your mom says, "I expect you to go to law school just like your grandfather and I did." It's that we tell ourselves a story that says that if we don't go to law school, our family will disinherit us, never talk to us again, be permanently ashamed of us, etc.

The family may in fact roll their eyes at you because of certain actions you take. But what if you develop a Generous Hustle that makes you feel alive and is beautiful, significant, and fulfilling? Would that be worth the cost?

You decide if you want your life to be ruled by fear of what others say about you or if you're the CEO of your New Life. If you let them win, you're choosing to lock yourself up and give them the keys.

The world needs your Generous Hustle. You need your Generous Hustle to feel alive.

Not having the time

I'm working two jobs to put food on the table for these kids, and I don't have a spare second to do anything else.

What can you stop doing to make room? What can you start doing more efficiently?

"They say that in prison, you don't have any choices. Well, today you have a choice. You choose whether you stay here in this gym and want to be in Defy. If you want to die a criminal, get out because I don't want you here. I don't want to have to hustle up dollars for you if you're a con, because nobody likes criminals. I tell the world that you're a changed man who is ready for a second chance. If you're in, you better be really in, because I'm all in.

"Now I'm going to turn my back, and you walk out of here if you're not 100 percent in. If you stay, we're getting real. Stay at your own risk."

One of the most notorious gang leaders walks out. Thirteen other guys follow him. Like ducks.

"Did they have to leave?" I ask the correctional officer.

> *They would have gotten stabbed by their own gang members if they had stayed.*

I had just told them that if they stayed, they would have to bear-hug guys with a different skin color. The life-and-death risks of politics and pride got in the way of a second chance.

I told this story to a friend who was shocked that a guy who's been locked up for nearly 30 years would rather continue to choose prison ways over a second chance. I'm not shocked. The leader used his pride and prison politics as his excuse to not reinvent himself.

What's yours?

What values, pride, doctrines, or politics have you built your life on, and how are they working out for you? If any of these things aren't serving you well or are holding you back, what are you willing to walk away from?

Write down the things that are in your control that are separating you from your future.

———

Lane, a great friend and Defy volunteer, is back at my house. I love him, but if he complains one more time about how much he hates his top-dollar management consulting job ...

It was a broken tape for about two years. "I bet you'll still be in this job in a year."

> *There's no way.*

"I bet you'll still be in the job at Christmas."

Nope. I'm going to make a change before then.

"What's going to change that will make you make the change?"

I don't know. I just know that I'll shoot myself if I'm still in this job by Labor Day.

"Instead of shooting yourself, how about you put your money where your mouth is?"

I get Lane to promise, in writing, that if he doesn't leave his job before Labor Day, he will owe Defy $5,000.

It worked. The fear of losing $5,000 made him finally take the plunge.

At first, he plunged into nothing. He was unemployed for a few months. It was frightening and nerve-racking. But every day, instead of a full-time job complaining, his full-time job was finding a Generous Hustle that would fulfill him.

Three months later, he emerged on the other side of the pain and landed his dream job doing business development for an amazing company in the Bay Area.

Will it take a one-sided bet to motivate you to leap?

Defy will be happy to get your check in the mail (or better yet, see you achieve your Generous Hustle). ☺

FINDING YOUR GENEROUS HUSTLE

Where does one get started in the discovery process?

I didn't know what to read, and no one handed me a magical change-your-life book list. I didn't know what I wanted for my future, but I knew what I *didn't* want anymore.

It was time to start.

I was working 60 hours a week and had little spare time, so I invested my subway ride, 30 minutes each way, in reading. I committed one additional full hour per day to reading and studying. I forced myself to wake up early, even though I hate mornings.

Had I waited until I "found" the time, I wouldn't be doing what I'm doing today. Who finds time, anyway?

What do you need to read to grow? I made a list of heroes who inspired me. I read their autobiographies or biographies.

The autobiography of Martin Luther King Jr. had the deepest impact on me. He was only 27 when he started his movement. I was already 25; I had no time to waste! I gained courage from his courage, and allowed my heart to become enraged over racial and economic injustice.

Mother Teresa was a total badass. If a little old nun with no resources could do it, what excuses do we have?

They say that if you average the income of your five closest friends, that's probably what your income looks like. I'm guessing that the same is true for Generous Hustles and fulfillment. If your five closest friends are generally unfulfilled and stuck in ruts, you will probably stay in your rut, too. If your five closest friends took risks to get the lives they wanted, chances are you will get there, too.

If you don't know where to find friends who live inspiringly, start reading about the lives of those that have made a difference, immersing yourself in their habits and patterns, so you can become more like them.

———

Some aspiring entrepreneurs get paralyzed in the ideation process because they put pressure on themselves to come up with a genius idea. They think that if you want to start a business, you must have a patented idea, it must be super unique, and it must have enormous barriers to entry. So then, because you don't have a genius idea, you end up starting nothing, while deceiving yourself into thinking that you will get this perfect creative idea one day.

Seth Godin taught my EITs, "Reject the mythology that a business has to be innovative. Instead, figure out how to be useful—how to solve someone's problem and get paid for it."

At Defy, we have our EITs start simple cash-flow businesses—companies they can incorporate and get to profitability within three months, like painting companies or dog-walking companies. And we make them launch their businesses uncomfortably fast. As of 2017, we've incubated and funded 170 of our grads' fast-start businesses, and their companies have been so successful that they're our best fair-chance employers—they've hired nearly 400 other people who needed second chances!

The point is, stop trying to be so fancy. Just start simple and do something.

Almost every aspiring entrepreneur I know would stay in the "aspiring" bucket for life if his or her feet weren't held to the fire. The closer people get to the launch date, the more fear sets in, and the more likely they are to walk away from their dreams.

Why am I talking about business ideation? Because it's almost the same process as figuring out your Generous Hustle. If you wait to get going until you discover the next billion-dollar idea, you're never going to launch. If you wait until you figure out how to be the next MLK or Mother Teresa, you'll never start, because you're unlikely to do something that will become globally heroic.

Eric had waited three years for the surgery. He received the notice, finally. Only two more days.

Eric's jaw had been wired shut since the fight that broke it into pieces. He was ready to be able to open his mouth again, to be able to eat normal food and speak clearly.

The problem was that the surgery day was in conflict with the only exciting appointment Eric had had in ten years of incarceration: his Defy pitch competition and graduation. It would be his first time in a cap and gown.

He took a risk. He postponed the surgery, even though he could hardly speak through the wires.

He knew he had made the right choice when he placed first in our pitch competition—first out of 95 EITs. It was the proudest and best day of his life. Worth it.

How do you decide what to do when you have visions for your Generous Hustle that seem to conflict with one another, or visions that conflict with your reality?

You want to work overseas at a nonprofit, but you have kids in private school. Or you want to become an entrepreneur, but you're working 60 hours a week and need the income from your job to start your business, and you don't have time to start something if you keep working 60 hours a week.

How do you decide which vision is more important?

You can start with the end game—by actually writing your eulogy like my EITs do.

You can also start by writing out your top ten life values and then prioritizing those values. Is being a great parent more important than making more money? Is being healthy and fit more important than going back to school? Are fighting injustice and making a difference more important than being financially stable?

By age 25, I knew that one of my most important values was generosity. I feel significant and alive when I am generous with others. I like to give more than most people are comfortable with. Although I hadn't yet started PEP, I was living my Generous Hustle. I was giving away nearly 30 percent of my income, and it gave me great fulfillment and a reason to keep earning those paychecks.

What are your non-negotiable driving values in your life? If you make a list of ten values that are important, which three to five values will you never, ever compromise?

———

I so easily could have said no when my friend invited me to prison for the first time. I was searching for meaning and wanted to figure out my Generous Hustle. Prison work wasn't on my list. But as she spoke about the men she had met in prison, and how so many of them wanted nothing more than a second chance, I could feel my heart buzzing.

I'd said I was willing to do anything to figure out my life purpose. So I said yes.

I said yes.

That one word changed everything.

Think back to the most recent time your heart buzzed, and you ignored it. Maybe you watched a movie or read a book about something that really inspired you. Maybe it was a conversation with a friend. Maybe there was a natural disaster and you felt your heart buzzing about making a difference—but you ignored it.

Write down the five most recent times your heart buzzed and you ignored it. Maybe your list will contain things like this:

- Was asked to join the PTA

- Cried while watching the news of the homes burning down in the wildfires and thought about the homeless families

- Was invited to run a race that would raise money for cancer

- Could have brought toys to church for the holiday toy drive

- Was invited to a parenting class

- Was given a book on entrepreneurship that I have yet to pick up

- Was asked to forgive, but couldn't get myself to do it

- Watched a movie about foster kids and thought about learning more about being a foster parent

- Read a few chapters of this book and think Defy is pretty cool

Do you see a pattern on your own list?

Now write down the reason or excuse that stopped you from taking action on your heart buzz. Maybe your list will contain things like this:

- Got a text message from a friend; then forgot to look up the website

- Had another social event on my calendar

- Didn't want to disappoint someone else

- Busy, busy, busy—who needs another commitment?

- Forgot

- Fell asleep

- Out of sight, out of mind

- Someone else will take care of that family

- I have enough problems of my own

Any patterns with the excuses? Any patterns you're committed to breaking, so you can break out of your prison?

Remember, it's the feeling of safety or the magic of fulfillment. A or B. And if you don't interrupt some of these patterns, you're choosing A by not choosing B.

Before officially starting Defy, I wrote a business plan and showed it to a *Fortune* 500 CEO I really respected. He laughed me out of his office. I felt so humiliated for coming up with such a "stupid idea." I remember walking out of his office and down Fifth Avenue in New York with tears streaming down my face, feeling like a failure. Again. I was so close to giving up.

What if I had?

———

You might get close to starting your Generous Hustle. Maybe you'll see it, touch it, and come so close to victory, but the second the sacrifice gets a little more real, you'll want to quit. And you'll say, "That wasn't really my Generous Hustle after all." And maybe it was. But you will never know, because you walked away because you didn't have the stamina, couldn't keep a commitment, or stopped one inch before victory.

If we don't get better at commitment, our second chance might be for nothing. Fulfilling our commitments often requires sacrifice.

———

Does finding my Generous Hustle mean I will become "happy"? Depends on how you define happiness.

I'm living my wildest dream, but I'm unhappy a lot of the time. My Generous Hustle is hard. I am regularly unsuccessful and I get easily discouraged. I cry a lot (have I already said that?).

But my dream is not to be happy and carefree. My dream is to make a difference. I'm willing to keep going through the pain, and to make painful sacrifices, because it is worth it to me.

Earlier I talked about writing down your core values. If having fun is one of your priorities, then don't start an organization like Defy.

———

Do we really have to write a full plan before launching a new idea?

I'm a big fan of Eric Ries's Lean Startup methodology. He writes about the concept of an MVP—a Minimum Viable Product. What's the smallest, simplest experiment we can run to test the viability of our Generous Hustle, to see if we're on to something?

Old-school entrepreneurial thought was centered around writing long business plans and then using the plans to get investor buy-in. But this is a long, laborious, expensive process. Even when we think we have the most carefully crafted business plan, we see the errors when we launch.

Without even having heard of the "MVP" and "lean startup" terminology, I had MVP'd the concept for PEP before starting it.

I was about to return to the Texas prison for my second time as a volunteer. I had no idea what I was doing. I thought it would be fun to provide breakfast for the EITs. I didn't realize it would cost me nearly $1,000. So I asked my NYC private equity colleagues if they wanted to pitch in. For breakfast for Texas prisoners. I raised the money by going office-to-office.

I didn't really know how to fundraise. I hadn't incorporated PEP. I just did it—a little MVP test. And I learned that people were willing to entrust me with their money to make a difference.

At Defy, our EITs all run MVP experiments before they incorporate their businesses. Want to start a catering business? First host a dinner party and let honest friends decide if they want to pay for your food.

———

I didn't incorporate PEP as a nonprofit organization until after I had completed the first full class. The first class cost me about $10,000—something I could afford at the time.

I wondered if I would ever be able to get CEOs and executives to care. I didn't have a network in Texas. So when I got home from my private equity job, I wrote letters to 400 CEOs in Texas, inviting them to PEP's first-ever pitch competition. I figured handwriting would be more likely to get their attention than printed notes or email messages, so I scribbled notes to all 400 of them.

I received replies from 10 percent of them—40 CEOs.

I was on to something.

After my scandal and my resignation from PEP, I was sure that no warden would ever allow me back inside a prison. So for the first three years of running Defy, I served only men and women who had been released from prison.

Google had given us a large grant to scale our New York City work to the Bay area, and we had the unusual problem of having more money to use than we could find people to serve. So I decided we would MVP our work inside a prison.

State by state, I started cold-calling prison systems. CDCR (the California Department of Corrections and Rehabilitation) was the first to show interest.

It had been six years since I had stepped foot in a prison. I definitely felt out of practice.

I asked the CDCR if we could do an MVP-style focus group with some incarcerated men. I wanted to understand their needs and desires. I didn't want to assume that what worked in Texas prisons would work in California prisons. And I was insecure about my ability to lead again.

Stepping inside a prison again was the most exciting thing that had happened to me since starting Defy. As I was escorted into a class-room with 30 guys ready for us, I felt alive. They didn't know a thing about Defy or me, but they seemed happy to see me. I thought I would never see this day again. I felt grateful to be alive.

I hit Play on the introductory DVD about Defy and my story.

With all my healing work, I was sure I had overcome my shame. But there it was, back in full force, flooding my soul.

I was caught off guard by my newly returned shame. I had become accustomed to telling my resignation story to released men and women, and to audiences at speaking engagements, so why was I feeling this way again?

Because I couldn't stand the thought of my past screwing up my future, again. I was on the brink of greatness. My fear of getting kicked out, again, was mortifying.

Dr. Brant Choate, a Director of CDCR, was pacing in the back of the room as the video played. I was biting my nails off, knowing that the video was almost at the part where I revealed my sex scandal from years prior. And then the video got to my story. It was the first time I watched myself telling my own story. I cried in the corner.

About half of the EITs started crying. They turned back to look at me, almost in disbelief.

I've always feared the "really, you idiot?" looks. But these were looks of respect, looks of "we get it."

After the video finished playing, one of the guys said, "You're just one of us."

We all laughed. I realized that maybe my story was the best tool I had to break the ice. My pain showed them that I wasn't just some fancy white lady from New York City who wanted to steal their business ideas. I left my heart at Solano that day.

Within nine months, Defy was in 15 prisons and jails nationally.

Now it's your turn.

We've talked about spectatorship, commitments, and accountability. Are you inspired by all this talk about reinvention and generous hustling? Inspired ... to do what?

Here's your choice:

1. You can be a spectator on the sidelines and pretend this book is a novel.

2. Make the most of this. Commit to your own Generous Hustle, get an accountability partner, make a deal, transform your hustle.

Why not?

I didn't invent this process myself. This process came from the coaching I've received from the mentors and friends who have led me through my journey.

Trust the process, and I promise you transformation.

Trusting the process will require commitment. Commitment is strengthened by accountability.

The transformation isn't caused by the dream. It comes from the hustle. I not only tell myself I *will* do it; I also promise someone else I will do it by a certain date, or else there will be consequences. For instance, I will owe them money or will do a certain painful number of pushups if I don't deliver.

I don't know about you, but it's this accountability that pushes me through the open door. The work happens. If I just tell myself I want to do it? It doesn't happen.

I'm not here to make you comfortable. I'm here to make you better.

———

PLEDGE FORM

The dream is free; the hustle is sold separately.

By _____ (date),

I promise to tell my hardcore friend, _____
(accountability partner's name), **that I've kept my promise to do:**
(insert an achievable, measurable, quantifiable goal here)

_____

_____

_____ by _____ (date).

By fulfilling this promise, I will be: _____

_____

_____ (insert the outcome you anticipate).

If I break my promise, _____

_____(insert consequence).

If I keep my promise, _____

_____(insert reward).

_____   _____
Your signature   Witness signature

In or out. Your Generous Hustle can start now. If you let it.

Circle one:

I am out.   I am in.

What are people going to say about me now?

It was a year after my resignation from PEP. I was about to announce Defy, my Vision 2.0.

As I hit the Send button on the letter announcing my reinvention, I experienced some of the same unsettling feelings that I'd had when I'd hit the Send button on the resignation letter. My self-doubt was at such high level.

My EITs go through this every time before they incorporate their businesses.

I've failed so much. Could I handle one more failure?

It's so damn sexy to dream about dreams and starting something new. But actually doing it? The heat is on.

The heat had turned me wimpy.

But this wimp still hit the Send button. No one said you had to be fearless about the reinvention process. You can feel the fear and do it anyway.

Our EITs write out their own personal statements. And then they memorize the statements, and they say them aloud in front of our executive volunteers for feedback. These statements are 200 words or fewer, spoken from the heart in under two minutes; ideally, in 90 seconds. Try it.

State why you are awesomely qualified for the opportunity in front of you (whether it's a job, a date, an investment, or a mortgage). State three to five tangible qualifications or accomplishments that make you a solid candidate for the opportunity. Really sell yourself here, and if you're struggling, fake it 'til you make it.

Then admit you're human. "Unfortunately, I haven't always been on the straight and narrow. I made some mistakes _____ years ago."

Then sum up the consequences, but keep them vague. The interviewer/assessor can always ask questions later. One sentence on the consequences—not five minutes!

I served ten years in correctional facilities.

Then turn that corner, fast. Name three tangible things you've learned about yourself. Three specific ways you've changed—not "I'm a changed man," but:

I now meditate daily, coach my son's soccer team, and am enrolled in college.

Then three reasons the assessor will benefit if they give you a chance. Then:

I know you have many other options. If you take a chance on me, I promise you I will not only meet your expectations, I will exceed them. I promise I will make you proud.

Properly rehearsed and then presented to a parole board, this personal statement can get an EIT out of prison. It gets the parents of your new date to trust you. It gets VCs to decide if they're for real when they talk about valuing failure.

People frequently call me a "fearless leader." But if you could see inside my brain and my heart, you would see that I'm a scared little girl, just as terrified as anyone else—perhaps just as terrified as you are to break out of your comfort zone, which might be why you picked up this book.

My fear is there, same as for you. The is no difference. It takes courage to find the commitment. We have to muster up more courage every day.

I don't get this courage on my own, though—who said we needed to go at it alone?

———

Why do people say that "quitting isn't an option" when it always is?

Defy is just like my high school wrestling days. I was the only girl. When I started, I could hardly do ten consecutive pushups or one pull-up.

Every day at practice, the boys would beat me up so badly that I was thankful to have the entire girls' locker room to myself once the torture was over. I would cry, looking over my bruises and feeling completely defeated. I wanted to quit. Nearly every single day.

I just chose, every day, not to quit.

My whole first year of wrestling boys, I scored only two points. I owned my school's record for getting pinned the most and the fastest. Getting stacked was exceptionally humiliating. Looking back, it was the best resilience life training I could have had.

In high school, I won the California State Women's Wrestling Title for the 125-pound division. There were girls on nearly every other high school wrestling team in California, but most refused to wrestle boys. By the time I faced off in my first matches with girls, I had been strengthened by the torture from the strong boys.

Even though Defy posts huge successes, the day-to-day work feels just like the wrestling mat. I get stacked all the time and go back for more.

I think it's all of those bruises and losses that prepared me best to come alongside America's biggest underdogs, shine them up, and put them back in the fight for their own lives. The people I work with every day defy the odds and overcome the hugest obstacles and pasts. They inspire me to keep going when I want to quit the most.

Refusing to quit is different from wanting to quit.

It's so normal to want to quit. That's okay. Expect it.

I frequently remind myself, even now, that this work is my dream. I have been given a second chance. Not many people really live their dreams, and I'm living mine, and my dream is a difficult, tearful one. I sometimes despise and resent it, but it's my dream, and I didn't sign up for an easy one.

Doing the same old, same old—staying in our comfort zones—isn't scary. Our EITs are used to the dangers of the streets. And doing time isn't scary after you've gotten good at doing time for the past 20 years.

What's scary is doing something brand new, something where you could fail, and especially if you could fail publicly and face embarrassment.

For most of my guys, failure is actually quite familiar. Success is scary because it would be new. With success, they might have a whole new set of responsibilities.

PREVENTING FAILURE

John Montgomery asked me, "Do you have a crisis plan?"

I'm not sure why making mistakes after a failure is so common, but it is. On the rebound, we seek firm ground, often in the wrong direction, to our detriment.

If I want to avoid the rebound trap, I better have a solid crisis plan in place. A step-by-step plan to follow when I get in trouble, or when trouble is around the corner.

Our temptations, rebound mechanisms, and crisis plans are unique to each of us, but I'll share some of the steps that I formed as part of my crisis plan:

1. Don't make decisions when I feel mentally unstable.

2. Postpone all decisions possible while in crisis.

3. If I have to make a decision while in crisis, make only the smallest, least permanent, least consequential decision.

4. Call somebody to cry.

5. Call somebody for advice.

6. Check the advice I get with a few other friends.

7. Come clean, even on the small stuff.

Warden Rosemary Ndoh took the stage to welcome the volunteers to Avenal State Prison.

> *Thank you for coming today. We need you. My men are precious. Yes, they have made mistakes, very big mistakes. They will make more mistakes in their lives. But thank you for seeing them for the precious men that they are, instead of just seeing them as the label of their worst thought process, for a bad decision they made 20 years ago.*

A warden, calling her men "precious."

Everyone in the room was in tears. It was just 9 a.m.

To me, one of the most freeing parts of Warden Ndoh's words was this: "they will make more mistakes in their lives." She removed the impossible expectation of perfection. So many of us have it of ourselves, or of others. Like, okay, you screwed up, so now if you really learn your lesson, you better never do it again.

I know I've told myself that. But that tape invites more failure.

We've covered a lot of ground in this book—and if you follow these strategies, from identifying self-limiting beliefs and meditating on your self-freeing beliefs, to confessing, and forgiving, and grieving, and recovering, you'll be in much better shape. You might just feel whole again.

When we feel whole, we are less likely to self-sabotage. Especially if we are fighting for our new Generous Hustle—when we know we hold the keys to someone else's future.

But if you're even a bit crazy-driven or prone to excess like me, another important aspect of preventing failure is living sustainably. This is a lesson I've learned the hard way; balance does not come naturally to me. Balance is something I discipline myself into.

I used to beat my chest like other entrepreneurs do about sleeping four hours a night. Now I average eight hours a night. I track my sleep every day in an app, and I'm accountable for it. Studies show that when we don't sleep, our brains are more likely to make stupid decisions.

I nurture myself because I'm worth investing in. I carve out time for things I love, things that feel like a treat. I get a massage at least monthly. I have date nights with my husband. I spoon Nutella out of a jar as a reward. I have lots of nights, and even trips, with my girl-friends. I let my friends take care of me.

I engage in creative stuff because it makes me feel alive and not think about work. I sew most of my clothes. I take design classes. I cook. I paint. I study Spanish.

I go on silent retreats. I take a "monk day" one weekday a month and don't check email or my phone.

I work out four days a week, log it into an app, and pay someone a fine when I don't.

I take at least three weeks of unplugged vacation per year.

When I feel sad, I call people and cry out to them.

––––––

I've come to know my vital signs. When I ignore my needs, I look to get them met in unhealthy ways. That's human.

I've disrupted my previous hold-my-breath-and-then-explode pattern. Now I almost never feel like combusting. That used to be an all-the-time feeling for me.

I am nice to me because I deserve it and because I love me.

What are your vital signs? In what areas of your life are you most likely to implode?

If you were your own guardian angel, what would you have you start or stop doing in order to live in a more sustainable way, so you can prevent failure and hit success more often?

What can you change to love you, too?

HINDSIGHT

It took my losing everything I had to realize who I really am and know what gifts I have to offer to the world. I had to be stripped of my identity and credentials to learn to love myself and to allow myself to be loved and nurtured by others.

Maybe you can't imagine a better future yet. That's okay—trust the process; follow the baby steps in this book. I know you can get there. My EITs get there every day.

Defy is my second chance to give second chances. I would never have imagined that I would get to lead again, that I would get a second chance at being a wife, that I would have another opportunity to be so free.

I live for the moment at our incubator events when our EITs' kids say:

I'm so proud of my daddy and I want to be just like him. I'm going to take over my daddy's business one day.

I wouldn't see any of this if others hadn't seen my potential first, and if they hadn't loved me back to life when I felt lifeless.

Who will you be once you give yourself another chance?

Who will those closest to you be once you give them a second chance?

Who could we be as a country if we lived up to being the land of second chances that we are touted to be?

Defying the Odds
By Michael

Can we forgive—what would it take?
Imagine livin' life by your worst mistake
Let that sink in, resonate
Imagine livin' life by your worst mistake
Story of my life, makin' bad decisions
I was just / 21 when I came to prison
I thought years of my life going down the drain
I gotta, gotta rise, overcome this pain
Then I heard / talk / of the work you do
Leadership. Management. Entrepreneur training too.
Defy Ventures sounds too good to be true
I'll never forget when Sara Lizette and Danielle came through
Let's change a mind, change the world, take a stance
Let's warm 'em up with bear hugs and a dance
With Step to the Line you helped me see
Both sides of these fences house people like me
You sold me a partnership, not pity
Not a handout, this ride ain't free
You asked me to stand / and exercise my voice
It was / in that moment I made my choice
I chose health / and to stay true to me
I chose to be CEO of My New Life
I chose to be free

There's a thousand-word essay to start for short
Then / twice a week we had to report
Loggin' / 12 hours in class a week
There's plenty of work / you're gonna skip some sleep
So / show up early and grab a good seat
Your video courses taught me / so many lessons
Like Henry Cloud on overcomin' depression
First day of class / I didn't know what I'd stepped in
Took a / gang of notes and I'm glad that I kept them
There / are a couple things / that I would never knew
Like / you write a resume / just to get an interview
A bad plan's better than no plan at all
Resiliency is key, you gotta rise when you fall
Remember / the load won't break you / it's how you carry it
You taught me financing on down to etiquette
I got my fork and my knife
Split from my left to my right
And Ima do what you do / cuz you're the host for tonight
Defy Ventures has changed my life / If I could
Go back / man, I'd do it twice
You've helped me grow / in so many ways
Now when I look in the mirror / I say I love you each day
CEO of Your New Life / that's the name
Transform your hustle / Transcend your pain
Thank you Catherine, you changed the game
Now it's time for me to do the same

ACKNOWLEDGEMENTS

If you've had anything to do with our incredible Defy journey, bringing this book to life, or my own second chance, on behalf of the entire Defy family: we love your guts.

I'm in awe of the influencers who have our backs. These acknowledgments are lengthy, yet not lengthy enough. They're straight from the heart, because those of you who sacrifice for Defy don't do it to get your name on a plaque; you do it because you're action-takers who are building the kind of country we want to live in.

Thank you, Sheryl Sandberg, for writing the foreword and for being a friend, role model to me, and tremendous supporter (and for launching Defy in a women's prison!). Thank you to each leader who provided credibility to our effort by writing blurbs for the book.

Unlimited thanks to the thousands of individuals, foundations, and companies that have supported Defy with their volunteer efforts and donations. You can see our honor roll at defyventures.org/honorroll. To our earliest, pioneering funders who believed in my ambitious vision even when Defy was itty-bitty: thank you for betting on me and for prioritizing criminal justice reform. To José Zeilstra: where would I be had you not invited me on that first prison visit in 2004? Thank you to you and David Kidder/Bionic for the unyielding moral support, connections, and funding for twelve years!

To the hundreds of fair-chance employers who have hired released Defy grads: thank you for modeling, to the world and to your own employees, what corporate social responsibility looks like. Thank you for proving to my incarcerated EITs that there is a legal, viable pathway; that they are wanted and are valuable to you.

To those who invited me on your stages: thank you for giving us the platform to create a movement. YPO Global, TEDx, Google, Entrepreneurs' Organization (EO), The Economist, Fast Company, SOCAP, Upfront Summit, WIRED, and so many great universities including Harvard, Stanford, Princeton, and UNC.

To my long-time friend Gary Carini at Baylor, and the entire board of Baylor University's Hankamer School of Business: thank you for vetting Defy's curriculum and for finding it worthy of your prestigious Baylor MBA certificate. Earning your certificate means the world to our EITs and makes their families so proud.

To the faith-based community that has embraced our mission, had me speak at their churches and conferences, funded scholarships, provided volunteers, and covered our work in prayer: thank you for being first-responders when it comes to grace. Willow Creek Church, Lower Manhattan Community Church, Reality Church, Forefront Church, Fairfax Community Church, Blue Conference, Redeemer Church, Newsong Church, and Catalyst.

To the venture capitalists, companies, and universities that have hosted Defy EIT field trips at your offices: thank you for turning us into a super-cool startup incubator and for providing opportunities to our EITs that other entrepreneurs would chew their arms off to have. Union Square Ventures, Goldman Sachs, Sequoia, Kleiner Perkins, Andreesen Horowitz, Stanford GSB, Harvard Business School, LinkedIn (Jeff Weiner), Facebook, Google.org, Google X, Rocket Lawyer, eBay, Box, Redpoint Ventures, Wix, and NYSE.

To Jacquelline Fuller and Justin Steele of Google.org—it's your "fault" that Defy is national. Thank you for your love of social justice and grace, and for being the first to recognize that our good work in New York City had to exist nationally, and for bringing us to California. And to Mike and Dot Bontrager, who took a huge bet on us by providing risky funding that turned Defy from a brick-and-mortar classroom model that served 50 people per year, into a scalable blended learning model, allowing us to now share our curriculum with tens of thousands of incarcerated people nationally.

To our prison partners and wardens: if only the world could see your hearts for rehabilitation and your thankless sacrifice on behalf of our incarcerated citizens. You care even when the world thinks you don't. Secretary Scott Kernan and Director Brant Choate (CDCR) and Director Scott Frakes (Nebraska DOC), you have changed my life. Your courageous leadership inspires me. Thank you to each of you for being a light in the world.

To all who serve on Defy boards (including our national governing board, national advisory board, and our local boards in New York, Nebraska, San Francisco, Los Angeles, San Diego, and Colorado), thank you for your leadership and for raising the money that allows Defy to scale. To our Executive Council, thank you for using your influence to open huge doors: Sheryl Sandberg, Preet Bharara, Mark and Louise Holden, Brad Feld, and Seth Godin.

To my friends and mentors who stand by me even at my lowest points: I wouldn't be here without you. Rod Washington, Bill and Andrea Townsend, John Montgomery, Julie Priest, JC Chang, Charles Brown, Joe Moglia, Danielle McMorran, Dave Crenshaw, Beth Valente.

To Dan and Aileen Tocchini, Dana Heartman, Troy Elmore, and Dr. Henry Cloud: thank you for teaching me so much of what I've learned and adapted for Defy's personal growth and character development exercises (some are described in this book) and courses.

To our brave EITs, particularly those who shared their stories for this book—thank you for modeling redemption for all of us. (All names of EITs used in this book are real, with the exception of the following: Roland, Brian, Ray, Kian, Joey, Carter, Rudy, Joe, Cody, and Marco.) So many more EITs contributed stories that I sadly didn't get to include in this book; go to defyventures.org/stories if you just can't get enough!

To my staff, who tirelessly devotes themselves to the "making of the sausage." We can make Defy look glamorous, but to each of you who have given your lives to this mission: thank you for loving hard even when it's inconvenient, annoying, expensive, and exhausting. Thank you for enduring the hard stuff to break through to the amazing.

To my husband, Charles, for partnering with me in this mission, and for sacrificing dearly for our Defy Family. For comforting me when I return home from a week in prison and for holding my hand when I cry as I process all the pain I see every day.

To the team who produced this book: thank you to Alex Peck, Creative Director, who turned this work into something beautiful, and to Maya P. Lim, Associate Designer—for not just doing your job, but for investing yourself in every detail. And to Tom Kubik, my good friend and all-time favorite Defy photographer for shooting the book cover photo (for free) and for the humanizing portraits and photos you've taken of our EITs (some of which I've included in this book).

And finally ...

I love the man who pushed me to the finish line.

The journey of writing this book has been a challenging act of love for me. I found myself in tears every day as I wrote, as I poured my heart into these pages through raw stories of my inspiring EITs.

The man's name is Seth Godin, and I feel like a total spoiled brat for having this legend as my dear friend, mentor, and role model. He has supported Defy Ventures for years now. He is the ultimate Generous Hustler.

Defy's day-to-day needs tugged at my heart and calendar, yet Seth kicked my butt every time I resisted and postponed my writing. The truth is, I was scared, and still am, to produce something that feels so permanent and imperfect.

Seth helped to shape my ideas and stories. Out of his own pocket, he funded every single bit of this book's creation, so that every dollar from the sale of this book goes to creating life-giving second chances for Defy's EITs, instead of lining someone's pockets. He designed the cover with his Creative Director, Alex Peck. Seth is serving as the book's publisher and promoter, and he bought and donated more than 10,000 copies to give back to Defy.

Seth has been so instrumental to this book, to my leadership, and to my self-confidence, that I wanted his name on the cover along with mine, but he refused. He wanted Defy to stand by itself, instead of riding on his coattails.

Seth is good at getting what Seth wants, but so am I, and I told him I wouldn't let this book go to print if I couldn't include this acknowledgement of his sacrifice.

Seth, of everything you did for me in this journey, the most powerful gift was that you believed in me, unceasingly, and you pounded your faith in me into my stubborn brain every step of the way. When I submitted drafts that I thought were crap, you told me that my voice mattered. You taught me to stop dragging myself through the mud as I relived my pain.

You made me feel clean, and forgiven, and beautiful, and significant.

You led me to believe that my book could change the world, and that these stories would be a blessing to my readers, so that they might start to believe in themselves, too.

For having my back, and my EITs' backs, thank you forever, Seth.

My hope for you, the reader, is your freedom. Freedom from the shame that has incarcerated your mind and your heart, freedom from unforgiveness. My hope is for your second chance, and for childlike joy, as you too become the CEO of Your New Life.

Cat

WHAT KEEPS ME UP AT NIGHT?

Please, Catherine, I've needed Defy all my life! If you just give me a chance, I promise I won't let you down.

I walk into a new prison for a Kickoff. There are 200 wide-eyed guys in the gym.

You got my letters, Catherine?! I've been writing you for six years, praying you would finally bring Defy here! God really does answer prayers! I've been locked up for 20 years, and I haven't gotten access to any programs. Defy is my life dream!

Reality #1: I didn't read his letters.

I don't get to personally read the stacks of jail mail that we receive from near-hopeless people, begging for a second chance. My staff reads them, and when they respond, the incarcerated person often writes back, "Thank you so much for acknowledging that I exist! I can't believe you responded!"

Reality #2: I have only enough funding to serve 100 EITs at this new prison.

But 200 attentive, courteous, hungry men are in the gym. They saw the "Transform Your Hustle" flyer in the chow hall. They ignored their "this sounds too good to be true" hunch, took a risk, and allowed their hope to get ignited anyway. They show up with their best I'll-do-whatever-it-takes faces.

I cry myself to sleep that night, in frustration, as I visualize the sea of faces of the men who will be put on a waitlist. Our waitlists are painfully long. And that's painful from my perspective.

Can you imagine if you were the one locked up, waiting, waiting, and waiting ... just for a chance at any rehabilitation program?

You can change this with me. It's why I'm writing this book. I give my everything every day. I will continue to, but I'm not scalable. I need you.

Who are we to deny people the opportunity to transform, when they're pleading for a chance and are willing to do anything to prove themselves?

Will you join me in using our privilege to create opportunity and access for America's most committed underdogs?

WE NEED YOU

To provide a $500 scholarship for an EIT,
please visit www.defyventures.org/donate
or mail a contribution to:

Defy Ventures
5 Penn Plaza, 19th Floor
New York NY 10001

If you or a loved one has a criminal history and you are interested in enrolling in our program, CEO of Your New Life, we have a correspondence program that can be taken from anywhere in the U.S. Write us at the address above. We have a limited scholarship fund that we are expanding to serve more people, or go to www.defyventures.org.

If you would like to volunteer with Defy,
go to www.defyventures.org.

To have someone from Defy come speak at your company or organization, email cat@defyventures.org.

PHOTO CREDITS

Graduation photo on the back flap of the jacket by Debbie Bohan

EIT portraits on following pages by Tom Kubik